PlainBibleStudyGuides

PROVERBS

Study Guide

Material by Andy Sochor

"My son, give
attention to my
words; incline your
ear to my sayings."
Proverbs 4:20

Adult Class Material I 14 Lessons

Proverbs Study Guide, Second Edition
Copyright © 2021 by Andy Sochor
First Edition Copyright © 2015

Published by:
Gospel Armory Publishing
Bowling Green, Kentucky
www.GospelArmory.com

Printed in the United States of America

ISBN: 978-1-942036-71-5

Table of Contents

"My son, give attention to my words;
incline your ear to my sayings."
Proverbs 4:20

Introduction to the Book of Proverbs

Many books have been written in which the author claims to be imparting some wisdom to his readers. What makes the book of Proverbs different is the author and the source of his wisdom.

The Author of Proverbs

The last two chapters of Proverbs are attributed to *"Agur the son of Jakeh, the oracle"* (30:1) and *"King Lemuel, the oracle which his mother taught him"* (31:1). The identities of these individuals are uncertain. However, the bulk of Proverbs can be attributed to *"Solomon, the son of David, king of Israel"* (1:1). Some of these *"proverbs of Solomon"* were *"transcribed"* by *"the men of Hezekiah, king of Judah"* (25:1).

It is important that we understand how Solomon acquired his wisdom. We find the answer to this shortly after Solomon established his rule as king over Israel.

"In Gibeon the Lord appeared to Solomon in a dream at night; and **God said, 'Ask what you wish Me to give you.'** *Then Solomon said, 'You have shown great lovingkindness to Your servant David my father, according as he walked before You in truth and right-eousness and uprightness of heart toward You; and You have re-served for him this great lovingkindness, that You have given him a son to sit on his throne, as it is this day. Now, O Lord my God, You have made Your servant king in place of my father David, yet I am but a little child; I do not know how to go out or come in. Your ser-*

*vant is in the midst of Your people which You have chosen, a great
people who are too many to be numbered or counted. **So give Your
servant an understanding heart to judge Your people to discern
between good and evil.** For who is able to judge this great people
of Yours?'*

*"It was pleasing in the sight of the Lord that Solomon had asked
this thing. God said to him, 'Because you have asked this thing and
have not asked for yourself long life, nor have asked riches for yourself, nor have you asked for the life of your enemies, but have asked
for yourself discernment to understand justice, behold, I have done
according to your words. **Behold, I have given you a wise and
discerning heart, so that there has been no one like you before
you, nor shall one like you arise after you**"* (1 Kings 3:5-12).

It is certainly true that no one could equal Solomon in terms of wisdom.
When the queen of Sheba heard of Solomon's wisdom and traveled to visit him
in order to see for herself if the reports were true, she discovered that they were
absolutely true.

*"Then she said to the king, 'It was a true report which I heard in
my own land about your words and your wisdom. Nevertheless I
did not believe the reports, until I came and my eyes had seen it.
And behold, the half was not told me. You exceed in wisdom and
prosperity the report which I heard'"* (1 Kings 10:6-7).

God promised to give Solomon wisdom. When He did, the evidence of this
wisdom was so overwhelming that a ruler from another land confirmed that
Solomon's wisdom was far greater than anything she had been told about him.

Solomon's wisdom was miraculously granted to Him by God. This is not
going to happen to us today. It will take more time and effort on our part, but
we can certainly gain wisdom. Notice what James wrote:

"But if any of you lacks wisdom, let him ask of God, who gives to all generously and without reproach, and it will be given to him. But he must ask in faith without any doubting, for the one who doubts is like the surf of the sea, driven and tossed by the wind" (James 1:5-6).

After Solomon was given wisdom directly from God, he wrote down his wise teachings of the book of Proverbs. Why? If God would miraculously grant everyone wisdom who desired it, this written volume would be superfluous. He wrote these things down so that others could read them and receive instruction in the ways of wisdom.

It is important to note that even though Solomon was given wisdom directly and miraculously from God, he still possessed the characteristics necessary to receive wisdom – characteristics we must have if we wish to gain wisdom:

1. **Solomon recognized God as the source of all blessings.** When God asked Solomon to ask Him for what he wished, the king's first response was to acknowledge God's great blessings up to that point. *"You have shown great lovingkindness to Your servant David my father"* (1 Kings 3:6). If we hope to gain the wisdom that comes from above, we must also recognize what James wrote: *"Every good thing given and every perfect gift is from above, coming down from the Father of lights"* (James 1:17).

2. **Solomon was humble.** Though he had become king, Solomon recognized that he was *"but a little child"* who did not *"know how to go out or come in"* (1 Kings 3:7). We, too, must possess humility if we are to gain wisdom. We *"acquire wisdom"* by heeding the *"words"* of those who are teaching us of the wisdom that comes from above (4:5). James said that *"in humility,"* we are to *"receive the word implanted"* (James 1:21).

3. **Solomon appreciated his responsibility.** Solomon recognized that he was ruling over *"a great people"* that had been *"chosen"* by God (1 Kings 3:8). The enormity of his responsibility, coupled with his humility noted in the previous point, caused him to realize that he needed wisdom and to desire it.

4. **Solomon was selfless, putting others first.** Solomon could have asked God for long life, riches, or the life of his enemies (1 Kings 3:11); but he did not. Instead of asking for something that would be of primary benefit to himself, he asked for something that would benefit others – *"an understanding heart to judge [the] people"* (1 Kings 3:9). The wisdom of the world focuses on self-promotion and self-preservation. The wisdom that comes from above causes us to seek the good of others as we are told to love our neighbors as ourselves (Leviticus 19:18; Matthew 22:39).

If we possess these characteristics that Solomon demonstrated when he was granted wisdom by God, we will also gain wisdom as we follow the source of wisdom.

However, there is another important lesson to be learned from Solomon. We can learn from his example that the pursuit and possession of wisdom alone is not enough.

> *"Now King Solomon loved many foreign women along with the daughter of Pharaoh: Moabite, Ammonite, Edomite, Sidonian, and Hittite women, from the nations concerning which the Lord had said to the sons of Israel, 'You shall not associate with them, nor shall they associate with you, for they will surely turn your heart away after other gods.' Solomon held fast to these in love. He had seven hundred wives, princesses, and three hundred concubines, and his wives turned his heart away.*

"For when Solomon was old, his wives turned his heart away after other gods; and his heart was not wholly devoted to the Lord his God, as the heart of David his father had been. For Solomon went after Ashtoreth the goddess of the Sidonians and after Milcom the detestable idol of the Ammonites. Solomon did what was evil in the sight of the Lord, and did not follow the Lord fully, as David his father had done. Then Solomon built a high place for Chemosh the detestable idol of Moab, on the mountain which is east of Jerusalem, and for Molech the detestable idol of the sons of Ammon. Thus also he did for all his foreign wives, who burned incense and sacrificed to their gods" (1 Kings 11:1-8).

Solomon knew better. He possessed wisdom in the ways of God. Yet he did not use this wisdom. Instead, he ignored the will of God and followed the godless influence of those who were close to him. It is not enough to *pursue* wisdom, or even to *possess* wisdom; we must *use* the wisdom we have.

The Subject Matter of Proverbs

Under the broad category of *wisdom*, the book of Proverbs discusses many different subjects. It deals with the pursuit of wisdom itself. It includes practical instruction for living. It discusses matters relating to personal growth, our dealings with others, proper conduct in society, and appropriate service to God. These subjects are scattered throughout the book. This material arranges the various proverbs according to topic in order to help us in our study of the book.

The book of Proverbs breaks down into four basic areas:

1. **The *appeal* of wisdom** – This is done in two ways. First, the wise man *appeals* to his son to heed his words of wisdom: *"Hear, my son, your father's instruction and do not forsake your*

mother's teaching" (1:8). Second, wisdom is personified and makes an *appeal* for man to follow after her: "*Wisdom shouts in the street, she lifts her voice in the square*" (1:20).

2. **The *appreciation* of wisdom** – Once we recognize the *appeal* of wisdom, this second part explains why we are to listen by telling us to *appreciate* wisdom. This is done by pointing out the benefits and blessings that come when we follow after wisdom: "*Riches and honor are with me* [wisdom, see 8:12], *enduring wealth and righteousness. My fruit is better than gold, even pure gold, and my yield better than choicest silver*" (8:18-19).

3. **The *acquisition* of wisdom** – After hearing the *appeal* of wisdom and learning why we should *appreciate* wisdom, we will see instructions and encouragement that will lead us to *acquire* wisdom: "*Acquire wisdom! Acquire understanding! Do not forget nor turn away from the words of my mouth*" (4:5). "*The beginning of wisdom is: Acquire wisdom; and with all your acquiring, get understanding*" (4:7).

4. **The *application* of wisdom** – Simply acquiring wisdom is not the goal. Wisdom must be put into practice. Solomon says, "*Doing wickedness is like a sport to a fool, and so is wisdom to a man of understanding*" (10:23). A fool is not just one who lacks wisdom. A fool also *practices* wickedness. In the same way, one who has *understanding* will *apply* his wisdom and put it into practice.

How to Interpret Proverbs

When we study the book of Proverbs, we need to understand that it contains general statements about life. It is not talking about absolute rewards, punishments, or consequences that exist in this life that come as a result of either *wise* living or *foolish* living. Notice just a couple of examples:

"*Train up a child in the way he should go, even when he is old he will not depart from it*" (22:6). This statement is *generally* true. However, we all know godly parents who did all they could in raising their children the right way, only to have their children forsake the Lord after they had grown. Every person has free will. Sadly, some choose to forsake the good instruction they received from godly parents and follow a path which they should not go.

"*He who tills his land will have plenty of food, but he who follows empty pursuits will have poverty in plenty*" (28:19). Again, this is a statement that is *generally* true. However, there are occasionally times of drought, sickness, injury, or other hardships that might prevent the diligent worker from enjoying the fruit of his labor.

As they pertain to this life, the rewards, punishments, and consequences mentioned in Proverbs are *generally* true. However, if we follow the wisdom that comes from above, the reward we have to look forward to later is *absolutely* true. Solomon says, "*The righteous has a refuge when he dies*" (14:32), and wisdom "*is a tree of life to those who take hold of her*" (3:18).

In interpreting Proverbs, it is also important to remember what Solomon says near the beginning of the book:

> "*The fear of the Lord is the beginning of knowledge; fools despise wisdom and instruction*" (1:7).

If we pursue divine wisdom in the fear of the Lord – respecting Him enough to trust Him and follow His instructions – we will certainly profit from a study of the book of Proverbs.

Lesson 1

The Appeal of Wisdom

Key verses: Proverbs 3:1-4; 1:20-33; 8:1-11; 9:1-6; 8:22-36

The invitation to take hold of the wisdom that comes from above is universal. It is expressed in two ways in the book of Proverbs. First, we read of a father inviting his son to take heed to his words (4:20). Second, we read of wisdom personified extending the invitation for all to come, learn, and become wise (8:1, 4-6).

The Father's Appeal

Read: Proverbs 3:1-4

The father's instructed his son to *"not forget"* his teaching implies that his son had already been taught (3:1). The father is simply *reminding* his son of what he has instructed previously. The father's invitation then is for the son to *hear* and *accept* his teaching, *retain* his teaching (*"not forget"*), and *apply* his teaching (*"keep my commandments"*).

But why should the son listen to his father's instruction? He should listen, not just because of the authority his father has over him, but because he will benefit from heeding his father's command (3:2). The children of Israel were told, *"Honor your father and your mother, as the Lord your God has commanded you, that your days may be prolonged and that it may go well with you on the land which the Lord your God gives you"* (Deuteronomy 5:16). Similarly, the wise man tells his son that by *accepting, retaining,* and *applying* his teaching, he will be blessed for many years. This, of course, is *generally,* not *absolutely,* true.

The father again tells his son to *retain* his instructions (3:3). He can do this in two ways. To "*bind them around your neck*" suggests an outward manifestation of the son's retention of his father's teaching (actions, words). To "*write them on the tablet of your heart*" describes how his father's instructions were to govern his inward being (thoughts, motives). The point is that the wisdom the father imparts to his son, and the wisdom found throughout the book of Proverbs, is for the *whole* man (actions, words, thoughts, and motives).

The father mentions a twofold benefit of following his words of wisdom (3:4). First, his son would "*find favor...in the sight of God.*" As previously noted, a healthy "*fear of the Lord is the beginning of knowledge*" (1:7) and "*wisdom*" (9:10). One must follow after divine wisdom to be pleasing to God. Second, his son would be of "*good repute in the sight of...man.*" The application of the wisdom imparted by this father and discussed throughout the book of Proverbs is practical and can be easily seen and will be respected by others.

Wisdom's Appeal

Read: Proverbs 1:20-33

This is the first of three passages we will be considering in which the wise man personifies wisdom and describes her *appealing* to man to take heed to her.

The fact that Wisdom is being described as shouting and crying out in the *street*, in the *square*, at the head of the *noisy streets*, and at the *entry gates* to the city (1:20-21) is meant to show us that the call of Wisdom is made *publicly* and *openly* to all. Yet there is no mention of a crowd gathering around, eager to learn from the one proclaiming wisdom; only an inattentive refusal to receive wisdom (1:24-25). The lesson is that though Wisdom calls to all, not all will obtain wisdom. Therefore, if one does not grow in wisdom, it is because he has *rejected* wisdom, not because wisdom was inaccessible to him. We have already noticed the father imparting wisdom to his son (3:1-4). What if there is no father to impart wisdom? What if the father is unwilling or unable to teach his son? Though the son in such situations would certainly be at a disadvantage, there is still wisdom to be gained as it is calling out to all, openly and freely.

Incredibly, there are many people who prefer life without wisdom (1:22) – at least the *divine* wisdom that is being offered to them here. They "*love being simple-minded*" and "*hate knowledge.*" We often hear the phrase, "ignorance is bliss." To those who are willingly foolish and naive, this is their motto. They know just enough about the wisdom that invites them that they have convinced themselves that they want no part of it. Instead they "*delight themselves in scoffing,*" preferring to ridicule and mock rather than learn and grow. But why would so many people prefer simple-mindedness and foolishness over the wisdom that comes from above?

For one to abandon his foolishness in order to take hold of wisdom, he must first receive *reproof* (1:23). He must be shown how he is in error so that he can make correction and follow what is right. This key component in gaining wisdom – *reproof* – is uncomfortable and undesirable to many. People do not want to have their faults pointed out to them and be told that they must now do something differently. This is why many reject divine wisdom. As we will discuss more in depth later in this study, we can infer from this passage that we must be willing to listen to reproof, admit wrong, and make corrections in our lives. If we are willing to do these things, Wisdom says she *will* pour out her spirit on us and make her words known to us. If we apply ourselves to wisdom with the proper attitude, we *will* be able to acquire it.

God never forces anyone to hear, learn, obey, or grow. We must *choose* to do those things. In the same way, the wisdom that comes down from above will not be forced upon us (1:24-25). Wisdom will *call*, but we can *refuse*. We are free to *choose* to pay no attention to the appeal of Wisdom. But there will be consequences.

Wisdom is said to *"laugh"* and *"mock"* when trouble comes to those who refused to listen (1:26-27). To us, this may seem a little harsh. But it is no more harsh than the fool's rejection of the appeal that was made to him by Wisdom. Also, it is important to note that this *calamity* is spoken of as a certainty. The text does not say Wisdom will mock *if* dread and distress come; it says that Wisdom will mock *when* dread and distress come. There are negative consequences that come as a result of one rejecting Wisdom. The timing and severity of these consequences will vary, but the fact that they *will* come is a certainty.

When the consequences for rejecting Wisdom come, Wisdom will not be found by those who will suddenly be interested in acquiring it (1:28-30). We might wonder: if Wisdom was previously crying out, why will she refuse to answer when these people start calling on her and diligently seeking her? The reason is because *"they hated knowledge and did not choose the fear of the Lord."* They rejected the *counsel* and *reproof* of wisdom. We might then wonder: does God not allow one who had previously rejected Him and His wisdom to repent? Of course He does (cf. Ezekiel 18:32; 2 Peter 3:9). But even if one repents, he will still have to face the negative consequences of the choices he made prior to his repentance. Therefore, since these individuals rejected the wisdom that could have prevented their calamity, even a penitent heart would not deliver them from the *physical consequences* of their prior decisions. Acquiring wisdom is a process. If we forsake the appeal of Wisdom until we need wisdom, it will be too late. We must grow in wisdom *now* in order to prepare for the future.

When calamity comes, those who rejected Wisdom will have to suffer the consequences of their rejection (1:31-32). The seed that they sowed in foolishness will bear fruit. Those who rejected Wisdom will eat of this fruit (experience the negative consequences of their choices) and be *satiated*. This means they would be filled to the point of disgust, just as when one becomes sick from eating too much of an unhealthy food. The *"waywardness of the naive"* brings about death, reminding us again that ignorance is *not* bliss. The *compla-*

cency, or *prosperity* (KJV), of fools brings destruction. As long as they are content in their foolishness and naivete, they will develop no desire to seek after wisdom.

But just as there are negative consequences for rejecting Wisdom, there is also a reward for accepting Wisdom (1:33). More of the benefits of wisdom will be discussed later in the study. But here Solomon tells us that those who listen to the words of Wisdom will enjoy *security* and *peace* from the threat of calamity that would be against those who rejected Wisdom.

Read: Proverbs 8:1-11

"Does not wisdom call, and understanding lift up her voice?" (8:1). This question is rhetorical. Of course Wisdom calls and lifts her voice. As we have already noticed, this call is made *publicly*, indicating that it is open to all (cf. 1:20-21).

Further emphasizing the need for all to take heed, we see that the wisdom that comes from above is intended for *"the sons of men"* (8:4). God expects people to gain wisdom and has made it so that all are able to do so. It is designed to give prudence and wisdom to those who are naive and foolish (8:5). Calling these ones *naive* and *foolish* is not meant to be an insult. Certainly all people, at some point in their lives, have a time when they are naive and foolish simply because they have not yet learned what they need to know. The point is that we should not *remain* in a state of naivete and foolishness.

The wisdom that comes from above is different from the wisdom of the world (cf. 1 Corinthians 1:20-21). Because man is fallible, the wisdom of the world is fallible. Paul would later write, *"For the wisdom of this world is foolishness before God"* (1 Corinthians 3:19). In contrast, because God is *infallible*, the wisdom that comes from above is *perfect*. As Wisdom describes her teaching (8:6-8), we see a *perfect* message that has come from an *infallible* being. Wisdom speaks of things which are *noble* and *right* (8:6). The word translated *no-*

ble or *excellent* (KJV) is used elsewhere to describe those in positions of civil or military power. It indicates that the words of Wisdom are *superior* over the worldly wisdom that is contrary to it. The lips of Wisdom speak *truth* and not *wickedness* (8:7). The teachings of Wisdom are wholly *righteous*, containing no hint of any error or foolishness (8:8).

Though the sayings of Wisdom as being wholly noble, right, true, and righteous (8:6-8), not everyone is going to accept the wisdom that comes from above as being these things. Many follow the wisdom of the world, believing it is more noble, right, true, and righteous than the wisdom that comes from above. Why do some reject godly wisdom for worldly wisdom? It is because they do not understand or have knowledge (8:9). One who truly understands and appreciates the difference between the two types of wisdom will always choose to follow after the wisdom that comes from above. Those who follow the wisdom of the world either do not *know* the wisdom that comes from God, or they have not put forth enough of an effort to *understand* it.

We will discuss more later in the study about the value of wisdom. The idea is introduced to us here (8:10-11). Those things which man values in this life – silver, gold, jewels, and any other desirable possession – cannot compare with the wisdom that comes from above. Therefore, Wisdom calls us to listen to her *instruction* and gain the *knowledge* that will lead one to acquire wisdom.

Read: Proverbs 9:1-6

The final passage we will notice that describes Wisdom's appeal presents a picture of wisdom making preparations to host a feast and inviting others to attend.

The fact that Wisdom has built a house (9:1), as opposed to pitching a tent, indicates that it is firmly established. The *seven* pillars (9:1) indicate *completeness*, that it is lacking in nothing. Preparations are made for this feast (9:2), and the invitations are sent (9:3). The call for men to attend the feast is done "*from the tops of the heights of the city,"* again, indicates a *public* invitation that is made to *all* (cf. 1:20-21; 8:2-3).

The invitation is directed to those who are *naive* and who *lack understanding* (9:4-6). Of course, all who lack wisdom from above need to answer this call. But one must be *humble* enough to recognize the fact that he is *naive* and lacking in understanding. Those who are rebellious or arrogant, though they are in need of godly wisdom, will not answer the call because they do not believe that they need it. We must be able to acknowledge our shortcomings and humbly seek after this wisdom. After one humbly receives wise instruction, he must repent (*forsake his folly*) and do the will of God (*proceed in the way of understanding*). It will not do any good for one to *learn* of the right way, then fail to give up his wickedness and follow after what is right. *Acquiring* wisdom must necessarily result in one *applying* wisdom. Most of the book of Proverbs is devoted to this *application* of wisdom.

The Timeless Nature of Wisdom

After considering the *appeal* of wisdom – both from a father and from Wisdom itself – it is important to consider whether or not this same wisdom is good for us today. The wisdom we are considering in the book of Proverbs is not *worldly* wisdom but wisdom that comes from above. As Solomon explains in the following passage, godly wisdom will *never* become obsolete or irrelevant. For this reason, Wisdom also appeals to us.

Read: Proverbs 8:22-36

Wisdom is timeless. It existed before, during, and after the Creation. The wise man explains in this passage why this is important.

Wisdom reminds us that the wisdom we are considering is not the worldly wisdom of man (8:22). Therefore, the wisdom that we are to pursue is older than the world itself. It belongs to God, not to man; so we must look to God and to what He has revealed in order to acquire this wisdom.

There are three periods of time mentioned in verse 23. First, there is the time *before* Creation ("*from everlasting*"). Second, there is the time *of* the Creation ("*from the beginning*"). Finally, there is the time in which man has inhabited the earth ("*from the earliest times of the earth*") – which has been since the sixth day at the end of the Creation week, right before God "*completed His work*" and "*rested on the seventh day*" (Genesis 1:26-2:2). This means that divine wisdom predates any human society or culture. Man often takes pride in how the culture in which he is a part has grown and progressed throughout generations, gaining collective wisdom along the way. Much of this wisdom, though, is *worldly* wisdom. *Godly* wisdom came before all of this, and so it is independent of human reasoning. Therefore, what may be considered "common sense" or some enlightened realization by a particular society – even our modern society – is not necessarily true or wise. True wisdom existed since before Creation, during the Creation, and from the beginning of man. In the following verses, Solomon expands on these time periods.

Before "*the beginning*" when "*God created the heavens and the earth*" (Genesis 1:1), God "*brought forth*" wisdom (8:24-25). This Wisdom that calls us to "*listen*" (8:32) is older than time. Therefore, we should not expect it to change with time.

Wisdom existed with God prior to Creation, then was used by God in creating the heavens and the earth (8:27-29). All that was created and continues to be sustained by His providence is a testament to the wisdom of God.

Wisdom is closely connected to God's work in Creation, being "*beside Him,*" with Him "*daily,*" and "*always before Him*" (8:30). This suggests that for us to possess true wisdom, we must acknowledge God as the Creator. To reject Him as the Creator is to reject the wisdom that existed "*beside Him, as a master workman.*" At the end, we learn that Wisdom's "*delight* [is] *with the sons of men*" (8:31, KJV). This wisdom exists for our benefit. The creation and subsequent providence, which are grounded in wisdom, are for our good. The divine message of wisdom that is revealed from above is for our good as well. As we continue this study, we will see many ways in which wisdom benefits those who follow after it.

Similar to what we have already noticed, Wisdom invites all to *listen*, *heed*, and become wise (8:32-33). Following this type of instruction must invariably lead to obedience. If we keep the ways of wisdom, we will be blessed. Conversely, if we neglect the ways of wisdom, then not only can we not expect the blessings, but we can expect negative consequences for this neglect. Not only must we gain wisdom, but we must regularly be reminded of the things which we have been taught so that, as the Hebrew writer stated, "*we do not drift away from it*" (Hebrews 2:1).

To be blessed we must *listen* to the words of Wisdom (8:34-35). Furthermore, we must exhibit patience and a willingness to wait daily upon Wisdom's instruction. Wisdom will never be obtained overnight. Therefore, we must diligently study so that we can have her teachings firmly planted in our minds. If we do this and follow after this wisdom, then we will find life and the Lord's favor.

While there are certainly benefits to following Wisdom, there are also negative consequences for rejecting her (8:36). When we forsake the wisdom that comes from above, we bring harm to ourselves and demonstrate that we "*love death*."

Questions on Lesson 1

1. Who/what are the two primary sources of the invitation for one to obtain wisdom?

2. What reasons does the father give for following after wisdom in 3:2, 4?

3. What is significant about the description of Wisdom shouting in the street, in the square, and at the gate (1:20-21)?

4. Why does Wisdom laugh at the calamity of the foolish (1:24-27)?

5. In what way is wisdom better than jewels, gold, and silver (8:10-11)?

6. Who is the source of wisdom and how long has wisdom existed (8:22)?

7. What is identified as the benefit of obtaining wisdom in 8:35?

Lesson 2

The Appreciation of Wisdom

Key verses: Proverbs 23:23; 3:13-26; 2:10-22; 3:5-8; 13:15

We have already considered passages discussing the *appeal* of wisdom. But why should we answer this call? There are many invitations that may be offered that are disregarded by those who are invited. Why should we listen to the *appeal of wisdom?* It is because of the great value of wisdom, the rewards that come from following wisdom, and the perils that we face when we reject wisdom.

All of these are pointed out to us in the book of Proverbs. When God offers His wisdom which was with Him from the beginning (8:22), He does not expect us to accept it without explaining *why* we should accept it. So let us consider the reasons why we should *appreciate* wisdom so we will heed the *appeal* of wisdom.

The Value of Wisdom

The first reason why we should *appreciate* wisdom is the inherent *value* of wisdom. But before we can consider the value of wisdom, we must begin with the starting point for pursuing wisdom – truth.

> *"Buy truth, and do not sell it, get wisdom and instruction and understanding"* (23:23).

We must first recognize that *truth* is more valuable than anything of a material nature which we could buy or sell. We should not understand truth to mean something subjective that will change from one person, time, region, or circumstance to another. Truth is the objective standard that has been revealed from God. It is the *word* of God (cf. Psalm 119:160; John 17:17).

Truth – the revealed word of God – is the starting point that leads to wisdom. The wise man also mentions *instruction* and *understanding* as coming from truth. This tells us three things about truth (the word of God):

1. It leads to divine wisdom.
2. It is the basis for all instruction in matters that pertain to God.
3. It can be understood.

Those who look for wisdom apart from the truth of God's word are seeking the wrong kind of wisdom. Those who use a standard of authority other than the truth of God's word for their religious practices and doctrines are in error. Those who believe that the truth of God's word cannot be understood are mistaken.

Truth leads to instruction. Instruction leads to understanding. Then understanding leads to wisdom. When man produces a product to be sold, the fair market value of it is always worth *more* than the sum total of the raw materials used to make it. Truth – God's word – is valuable. The psalmist described the words of God as being "*more desirable than gold, yes, than much fine gold; sweeter also than honey and the drippings of the honeycomb*" (Psalm 19:10). How much more valuable is the wisdom that comes from a proper understanding and practice of the truth. The following passages help us to understand just how valuable the wisdom that comes from above is.

Read: Proverbs 8:10-11, 18-19; 16:16

The first two passages have Wisdom speaking (8:10-11, 18-19), and the third contains a statement from the wise man about wisdom (16:16). The point is clear: wisdom is far more valuable than any riches of this world. Throughout history, gold, silver, and jewels have had a great value associated with them. It is natural, then, to see these as having great worth. But no matter how valuable these are, they "*cannot compare*" with divine wisdom. If we are to gain wisdom, we must value it so highly that we will not let even gold, silver, or jewels distract us from its pursuit.

The Rewards of Wisdom

Wisdom is not valuable simply because it has been arbitrarily declared to be valuable. It is valuable because of the rewards that come for following after it.

Read: Proverbs 3:13-26

The one who finds wisdom and gains understanding is *blessed* (3:13). But how so? The wise man explains how wisdom causes one to be blessed.

As we have already noticed, wisdom is of far greater value than the material things of this life. Of all the things we might desire, wisdom will prove to be far more valuable as a long-term investment (3:14-15). Elsewhere, in contrasting the wise and the foolish, the wise man writes, "*A man will be **satisfied** with good by the fruit of his words, and the deeds of a man's hands will return to him*" (12:14). We will be *satisfied* when we apply ourselves to wisdom and reap its fruits. Therefore, we should pursue it.

One of the benefits of wisdom, generally, is *long life* (3:16), as our lives are not cut short through foolish choices and activities. When we pursue the things that lead to wisdom – righteousness, humility, and the fear of the Lord – we find "*riches, honor and life*" (22:4; cf. 21:21). A few chapters later, Wisdom says, "*For by me your days will be multiplied, and years of life will be added to you*" (9:11). Riches and honor are also often byproducts of one's *acquisition* and *application* of wisdom. Wisdom says she will "*endow those who love me with wealth, that I may fill their treasuries*" (8:21; cf. 24:3-4).

Following after wisdom leads to pleasant and peaceful paths for life (3:17). Later, Solomon writes, "*The path of life leads upward for the wise that he may keep away from Sheol below*" (15:24). *Upward* is in the direction of heaven and the dwelling place of God. Therefore, the wisdom that comes from above shows us the way to reach God in heaven.

In the beginning, man's access to the tree of life was lost because of sin (Genesis 3:22-24). Wisdom is now "*a tree of life*" for those who follow after her (3:18) because, as we noticed in the previous verse, divine wisdom leads us back to heaven where the tree of life (eternal life) can be found (cf. Revelation 22:2). Elsewhere, the wise man writes, "*The fruit of the righteous is a tree of life*" (11:30). That which is produced by a life of righteousness, guided by the wisdom that comes from above, is eternal life.

The created world reflects the wisdom of God (3:19-20). This echoes the point that was made in Lesson 1 titled *The Timeless Nature of Wisdom* (pp. 12-13). Wisdom existed with God from before the Creation and was used by Him in creating the heavens and earth (8:22-29).

The father appeals to his son to keep hold of godly wisdom and understanding (3:21). It is not enough for his son to just listen and learn; he also needs to *retain* what he learned. He is encouraging his son to be clothed with wisdom and discretion (3:22). These teachings are to be "*a graceful wreath to* [his] *head and ornaments about* [his] *neck*" (1:9). In speaking of Wisdom, the father tells his son: "*Prize her, and she will exalt you; she will honor you if you embrace her. She will place on your head a garland of grace; she will present you with a crown of beauty*" (4:8-9). As one is *clothed* with wisdom and discretion, he obtains *life* for his soul (cf. 12:28).

One of the benefits of wisdom is the security and stability that one enjoys in life (3:23), as opposed to the volatile and uncertain life of one who rejects divine wisdom. "*He who walks in integrity walks securely, but he who perverts his ways will be found out*" (10:9).

Verse 24 mentions two benefits of wisdom. First, wisdom offers *security* (cf. 3:23). Second, following after divine wisdom allows one to have a good conscience, thus making his sleep *sweet*.

Even though one may be walking according to God's wisdom, there will be enemies that will rise up. However, if we follow after wisdom, we should take courage (3:25-26). There is *strength* in wisdom. "*A wise man is strong, and a man of knowledge increases power*" (24:5). "*A wise man scales the city of the mighty and brings down the stronghold in which they trust*" (21:22). Why is there such strength in wisdom? It is because this wisdom comes from the Lord. He is our *confidence*. As long as we stand with Him, we can be assured of triumph.

Read: Proverbs 2:10-22

Wisdom not only provides us with blessings for following it, but it also delivers us from evil. This is, of course, if we store up wisdom. Just before the passage above, the wise man says, "*He stores up sound wisdom for the upright; He is a shield to those who walk in integrity*" (2:7). The protection that comes with wisdom can only be realized if we pursue it. So these verses that talk about wisdom delivering us from evil assume that we have first *acquired* it. We will discuss the *acquisition* of wisdom later in the study. But understanding these benefits of wisdom shows us *why* we should work to acquire it.

A superficial knowledge of the instructions of the wise will not deliver us from anything. Wisdom must enter our hearts and souls if we want it to guard and watch over us (2:10-11). Therefore, we must be "*attentive to wisdom*" (2:2) and retain it in our innermost being. Only then can be expect wisdom to deliver us from evil and prevent us from doing things we will later regret.

In delivering us "*from the way of evil*," wisdom is designed to protect us from the influence of those who would lead us in this way (2:12-15). The first of these that the wise man mentions is "*the man who speaks perverse things*."

This man will try to lead us into sin by false teaching, lies, or verbal attacks. Second, there are *"those who leave the paths of uprightness."* They take pleasure in doing evil and will deviously try to lead others to follow after them. We are not to follow them or fall prey to them.

Wisdom also helps to deliver us from the dangers of the *"strange woman,"* or the *"adulteress"* (2:16-19). Much more attention is given to her later in the book of Proverbs (5:1-14; 6:24-35; 7:1-27; 9:13-18), and we will consider her more in a different part of our study. But we are told here that by following wisdom, we can avoid the ruin and damnation that comes from following the adulteress.

If we avoid the *"way of evil"* (2:12) and those who would lead us down that path, naturally we should expect to *"walk in the way of good men"* (2:20). We are going to keep company with one group of people – either the righteous or the wicked. Wisdom and righteousness are inseparable from one another. As wisdom delivers us from evil, it leads us in *"the paths of the righteous."*

The wise man reminds us at the end of this section of God's blessings and punishment (2:21-22). Those who through the instructions of wisdom live uprightly will be blessed. Those who reject wisdom and pursue wickedness will be rooted up.

* * *

"Where there is no vision, the people are unrestrained, but happy is he who keeps the law" (29:18).

The *vision* to which the wise man refers is the *revelation* (NKJV) that comes down from above, instructing us in godly wisdom. Without God's instructions, man is *"unrestrained."* Without His standard, there is no real standard for man to follow. While many foolishly believe that the absence of a divine standard is desirable, following the *"way which seems right to a man"* only leads to "*death*" (14:12; 16:25). One is "*happy,*" or blessed, if he "*keeps the law*" that has been delivered by divine revelation. Pursuing God's wisdom is for our benefit. Therefore, we must *trust God* and not ourselves and follow Him in all things.

> "*Trust in the Lord with all your heart and do not lean on your own understanding. In all your ways acknowledge Him, and He will make your paths straight. Do not be wise in your own eyes; fear the Lord and turn away from evil. It will be healing to your body and refreshment to your bones*" (3:5-8).

The Perils of Wickedness

After considering the value of wisdom, the rewards of wisdom, and the deliverance from evil that wisdom provides, we will next consider the *perils of wickedness* to further reinforce what we have already learned: embracing and following the wisdom that comes from above is for our good.

The *perils of wickedness* can be divided into three categories: hardship in life, lack of hope for the future, and the inevitability of judgment.

> "*Good understanding produces favor, but the way of the treacherous is hard*" (13:15).

The first peril of wickedness is *hardship in life*. People often complain about the way of God being difficult to follow. In one sense it is (cf. Matthew 7:13-14), but the path of wickedness contains hardships that can be avoided if one will simply follow what is right. The hardships that come as a result of one rejecting God's wisdom are unnecessary and avoidable.

One of the lies of sin is to convince us that we are still in control, rather than sin becoming master over us. But sins (*iniquities*) capture, or bind, us

(5:22-23). Paul later wrote, *"Do you not know that when you present yourselves to someone as slaves for obedience, you are slaves of the one whom you obey, either of sin resulting in death, or of obedience resulting in righteous-ness?"* (Romans 6:16). When we pursue sin, rather than righteousness or divine wisdom, we become *slaves* of sin. The end result is that we *"die for lack of instruction."* This shows us that God's *instruction* teaches us to repudiate sin. Many believe that sin is tolerable because it cannot cause a child of God to be lost. This idea is false. The word of God plainly teaches us to avoid sin (cf. Titus 2:12). Therefore, if one ignores this instruction and chooses to live without it, he will be captured by his iniquities, which will ultimately result in death – either physical death (as is Solomon's primary point) or, as we extend the application, spiritual death (Romans 6:23).

Related passages: Proverbs 6:12-15; 9:12; 18:3; 19:2-3; 21:27; 28:17.

> *"Do not fret because of evildoers or be envious of the wicked; for there will be no future for the evil man; the lamp of the wicked will be put out"* (24:19-20).

The second peril of wickedness is a *lack of hope for the future.* Any "benefit" that comes from following wickedness and worldly wisdom is only temporary. The Hebrew writer talked about Moses who forsook *"the passing pleasures of sin"* (Hebrews 11:25). While sin may seem appealing, it is certainly *passing.* There are no long-term benefits for sin.

After noting the fact that the wicked have no future to which they can look forward, Solomon tells us not to fret (worry) over them or envy them (24:19-20). It can be easy to worry and envy when we are too short-sighted to look at matters that extend past this life. Even if we see the wicked prosper in this life, we should not fret over them or envy them. No amount of prosperity in this life can compare to the great worth of the reward promised to those who will be faithful to the Lord (Matthew 16:26).

Related passages: Proverbs 11:29; 21:16; 22:8; 29:16.

"Judgments are prepared for scoffers, and blows for the back of fools" (19:29).

The third peril of wickedness is the *inevitability of judgment.* Judgment comes in various forms. One can be judged through the word of God as he is reproved by it (Hebrews 4:12). One can be judged in that he suffers the physical consequences of his error. One may also be judged by civil authorities when his wickedness is manifested in his violation of a just law. Finally, one stands to face God in judgment and receive punishment if his deeds are evil.

"On the lips of the discerning, wisdom is found, but a rod is for the back of him who lacks understanding" (10:13). The *rod* is a symbol of corrective discipline and is used throughout the book of Proverbs (13:24; 14:3; 22:15; 23:13-14; 26:3; 29:15). One who is *discerning* and displays *wisdom* does not need such correction. One who rejects wisdom and instruction must receive the *rod* in order to convince him to repent. This corrective discipline, when administered appropriately, is a sign that one has been judged as having transgressed the standard of righteousness.

Related passages: Proverbs 17:11; 19:19; 26:1, 8.

Those who foolishly follow the path of wickedness will suffer for it. There will be hardships in life. They will have no hope for the future. Those who are wicked stand to face divine judgment – both in this life and beyond – for their wickedness. In the end, it is far better for one to walk in wisdom than to walk after his own way.

To further emphasize the need for us to *appreciate* wisdom, we will turn our attention now to various passages in the book of Proverbs that highlight the contrast between the righteous and the wicked. We can divide these into two categories: *physical* consequences and *spiritual* consequences. The charts on the next two pages contain a list of these. As we consider the following passages, there will be a few that may have application to *both* physical and spiritual consequences; but for our study they have been placed in one category or the other.

Contrast Between the Righteous and the Wicked | *Physical Consequences*

Passage	Righteous	Wicked	Related
10:16	Wages of righteousness is life	Income of wicked is punishment	13:21; 15:6
10:24-25	Desire of righteous will be granted	What wicked fears will come upon	
11:3-8	Integrity of upright will guide them	Crookedness of treacherous will destroy them	28:18
	Righteousness delivers from death	Riches do not profit in day of wrath	
	Righteousness of blameless, smooth his way	Wicked will fall by his own wickedness	13:6; 29:6
	Righteousness of upright delivers him	Treacherous will be caught by their own greed	12:12
	Righteous delivered from trouble	The wicked takes his place	27:12
11:17-19	Merciful man does himself good	Cruel man does himself harm	
	He who sows righteousness gets true reward	Wicked earns deceptive wages	21:20
	Steadfast of righteousness will attain to life	He who pursues evil will bring about his death	
12:7-8	House of the righteous will stand	Wicked are overthrown and are no more	14:11
	Man will be praised according to his insight	One of perverse mind will be despised	
13:9	Light of the righteous rejoices	Lamp of the wicked goes out	
13:13-15	One who fears commandment will be rewarded	One who despises the word will be in debt to it	
	Good understanding produces favor	Way of the treacherous is hard	11:27; 12:21; 22:5

Passage	Righteous	Wicked	Related
13:17	Faithful envoy brings healing	Wicked messenger falls into adversity	
13:25	Righteous has enough to satisfy appetite	Stomach of wicked is in need	14:14
24:16	Righteous man falls 7 times, rises again	Wicked stumble in time of calamity	
28:25-26	He who trusts in the Lord will prosper	Arrogant man stirs up strife	
	He who walks wisely will be delivered	He who trusts in his own heart is a fool	

Contrast Between the Righteous and the Wicked | *Spiritual Consequences*

Passage	Righteous	Wicked	Related
3:33-35	The Lord blesses the dwelling of the righteous	The curse of the Lord is on the house of the wicked	12:2
	God gives grace to the afflicted	He scoffs at the scoffers	
	The wise will inherit honor	Fools display dishonor	
10:27-30	Fear of the Lord prolongs life	Years of the wicked will be shortened	
	Hope of the righteous is gladness	Expectation of the wicked perishes	14:32; 19:16
	Way of the Lord is a stronghold to the upright	But it is ruin to the workers of iniquity	
	The righteous will never be shaken	The wicked will not dwell in the land	12:3
11:20-21	The blameless in their walk are the Lord's delight	The perverse in heart are an abomination to Him	
	Descendants of the righteous will be delivered	The evil man will not go unpunished	
14:9	Among the upright there is good will	Fools mock at sin	

Passage	Righteous	Wicked	Related
14:22	Kindness and truth will be to those who devise good	Those who devise evil will go astray	
28:1	The righteous are bold as a lion	The wicked flee when no one is pursuing	
28:10	The blameless will inherit good	He who leads the upright astray will fall into his own pit	

Questions on Lesson 2

1. What do we get when we buy the truth (23:23)?

2. From what does wisdom deliver us (2:12-19)?

3. What is the "*vision*" without which "*the people are unrestrained*" (29:18)?

4. Explain the phrase, "*the way of the treacherous is hard*" (13:15).

5. What are the wages of the righteous and the wicked (10:16)? What New Testament passage is similar to this?

6. Why do fools mock at sin (14:9)?

7. Why are the righteous able to be *"bold as a lion"* (28:1)?

Lesson 3

The Acquisition of Wisdom

Key verses: Proverbs 1:7; 4:20-27; 10-13; 2:6-10; 3:5-7, 11-12

Now that we have considered the *appeal* of wisdom and can now *appreciate* the reasons why we should pursue wisdom, we turn our attention to *acquiring* wisdom. Once we know we need wisdom, how do we obtain it?

The Proper Approach to Acquiring Wisdom

In order to gain wisdom, we must have the right foundation. This means we start in the right *place* and have the right *mindset*, right *outlook*, and right *teachers*.

The *place* in which we must start if we hope to acquire wisdom is *in the fear of the Lord*. "*The fear of the Lord is the beginning of knowledge*" (1:7). "*The fear of the Lord is the beginning of wisdom*" (9:10). Without fearing God, there is no reason to listen to His instruction or follow after His wisdom. There is no motivation to do anything but what *we* desire. But if we fear the Lord, we will be motivated by what *He* desires.

The *mindset* we must possess starts with having good sense. This means that one *appreciates* wisdom and is willing to do what is necessary to acquire it. This is the opposite of the fool who disregards wisdom and does not want to do what is necessary to obtain it. Solomon asks, "*Why is there a price in the hand of a fool to buy wisdom, when he has no sense?*" (17:16). If one has "*no sense,*" there is nothing he can give in order to gain wisdom. And even if he were able to somehow "*buy wisdom,*" he would not know what to do with it once he had it. One must "*apply* [his] *mind to...knowledge*" (22:17; cf. 23:12) if he expects to grow in wisdom.

The *outlook* that we must have is one that expects continued growth throughout a lifetime. Our goal in obtaining wisdom will not be fully realized in young adulthood. Is it possible for a young man to have obtained a certain degree of wisdom in various aspects of life? Certainly. But we must be of the mind that we will continue to grow in wisdom at every stage in life. "*The glory of young men is their strength, and the honor of old men is their gray hair*" (20:29). The "*gray hair*" symbolizes *wisdom* that one has gained through a lifetime of experience. "*A gray head is a crown of glory; it is found in the way of righteousness*" (16:31). While young men might glory in their strength, they must be making efforts to grow in wisdom, even in their youth, so that when old age comes, they may be wise as God wants them to be.

The *teachers* from whom we must learn if we hope to gain wisdom must be wise themselves. "*He who walks with wise men will be wise, but the companion of fools will suffer harm*" (13:20). We cannot expect to become wise in the ways of God if we surround ourselves with those who will influence us in foolish and wicked ways. The wise man asks, "*Have I not written to you excellent things of counsels and knowledge, to make you know the certainty of the words of truth that you may correctly answer him who sent you?*" (22:20-21). The instruction from the wise man was designed to be taken and used by the one who was taught. We must have the right teachers – those who will instruct us of God's wisdom – if we hope to obtain this wisdom for ourselves. But what if one has no wise counselor to teach him? Is he then doomed to never being able to obtain wisdom? No, he can still obtain wisdom; but he must reject those who would direct him in foolish and wicked ways and follow the wise counsel found in the word of God.

And so, with the proper foundation, we have instructions to *acquire* wisdom.

Read: Proverbs 3:1-7; 4:20-27

The passages above emphasize the fact that wisdom is obtained through instruction that is passed from one to another – in this case, from a father to a son. We often talk about how wisdom comes with experience. This is true but not with experience *alone*. Wisdom is rooted in knowledge (3:1; 4:20). Knowledge is based upon what God has revealed (3:5-6). This knowledge of God's will must be bound about one's neck (3:3) and kept in one's heart (4:21), *"for from it flow the springs of life"* (4:23). With this knowledge, one turns from evil (3:7) and obeys the instructions of God (3:1).

Our determination to acquire wisdom must be wholehearted – trusting in God *"with all* [our] *heart"* and acknowledging Him *"in all* [our] *ways"* (3:5-6). We must remain focused, with our *"eyes* [looking] *directly ahead"* (4:25). We must be careful in our walk, watching *"the paths of* [our] *feet"* (4:26). We must be upright in all things – not turning *"to the right nor to the left"* and keeping ourselves *"from evil"* (4:27).

To Acquire Wisdom, We Must Listen

As wisdom is based upon instruction, it is therefore necessary for us to *listen* to wise counsel in order to acquire wisdom. So the wise father calls upon his son to *listen* to his words.

Read: Proverbs 4:10-13

Notice how the father tells his son to listen. *"Hear...and accept my sayings"* (4:10). *"Take hold of instruction"* (4:13). Elsewhere the wise man says, *"Listen, my son, and be wise"* (23:19), and *"Listen to your father who begot you"* (23:22). The goal in this listening is to *acquire* wisdom. *"Listen to counsel and accept discipline, that you may be wise the rest of your days"* (19:20).

This listening must be more than just *hearing* what is being taught. One may listen to a parent, teacher, or someone else who is trying to impart wisdom to him; but the words go "in one ear and out the other." He does not pay attention. He does not remember. And he certainly does not observe what was taught. We need to practice *real listening* if we hope to obtain wisdom. So the father says, "*Give me your heart, my son, and let your eyes delight in my ways*" (23:26). We have already noticed how the "*springs of life*" flow from the heart (4:23). Therefore, the instruction that we allow to be written on our hearts is the instruction that will have the greatest effect on our lives. So our listening must not be superficial and soon to be forgotten. We must absorb the wise counsel we receive into our innermost being so that wisdom can spring forth from our hearts to be manifested in our lives.

As we listen, we must also listen with a view toward *observing* what we learn. This is important because of the consequences of failing to do so – many of which we have already considered. The wise man says, "*He is on the path of life who heeds instruction, but he who ignores reproof goes astray*" (10:17). The wise counsel we receive must be put into practice if we hope to gain the rewards of wisdom.

> "*My son, observe the commandment of your father and do not forsake the teaching of your mother*" (6:20).

> "*For the commandment is a lamp and the teaching is light; and reproofs for discipline are the way of life*" (6:23).

This view toward observing what is taught is essential. Early in the book, Solomon writes, "*My son, if you will receive my words and treasure my commandments within you, make your ear attentive to wisdom, incline your heart to understanding... Then you will discern the fear of the Lord and discover the knowledge of God*" (2:1-5). Listening attentively, even to the point of *treasuring* commandments (and, by implication, striving to follow them), is necessary if we want to gain knowledge and grow in wisdom.

However, we must understand that there is a *right* way and a *wrong* way to listen. Let us first consider the *right* way to listen.

> "*Where there is no guidance the people fall, but in abundance of counselors there is victory*" (11:14).

Similar statements are made elsewhere in the book (15:22; 20:18; 24:6). It is dangerous to have "*no guidance.*" We need to have others to counsel us in the ways of divine wisdom. But Solomon does not just talk about one or two counselors to provide help but an "*abundance of counselors.*" It is good to seek guidance from multiple sources rather than putting complete trust in one man. After all, even our counselors may be mistaken from time to time. Therefore, it is helpful to receive instruction from several teachers. However, in doing this, we must heed the warning of Solomon: "*The naive believes everything, but the sensible man considers his steps*" (14:15). While an "*abundance of counselors*" can often be good, we must be careful not to believe everything we hear, lest we be like those of whom Paul later wrote who were "*carried about by every wind of doctrine*" (Ephesians 4:14). We must be careful that we accept godly wisdom and reject worldly wisdom (foolishness).

Related passages: Proverbs 12:15; 15:12; 16:20.

As there is a *right* way to listen, there is also a *wrong* way to listen. Let us notice a few passages that speak of this.

> "*The wise of heart will receive commands, but a babbling fool will be ruined*" (10:8).

We have already noticed that the wise are willing to *listen*. The fool, however, is not interested in *listening* but in *talking*. Solomon later writes, "*A fool does not delight in understanding, but only in revealing his own mind*" (18:2). Therefore, as a result of his unwillingness to listen, preferring to speak before he has understanding, he "*will be ruined.*"

"Wisdom is in the presence of the one who has understanding, but the eyes of a fool are on the ends of the earth" (17:24).

Again we see that understanding – which comes as the result of *listening* – leads to wisdom. Sometimes the fool is unwilling to listen because he is only interested in speaking (10:8; 18:2). Other times he may listen, but he does not listen well because he is distracted. His *"eyes...are on the ends of the earth,"* and he will not focus on the instruction that can lead to wisdom.

Related passages: Proverbs 23:9; 28:19.

To Acquire Wisdom, We Must Learn

Another step in *acquiring* wisdom is that we must *learn*. The knowledge that leads to understanding is available, both through the written word of God and the wise counsel that we receive from others. But the mere fact that knowledge is available does not mean we will automatically obtain it. We must *learn* it for ourselves.

If we are to *learn*, we must *seek to learn*. That is, we must have a desire to learn.

"The mind of the intelligent seeks knowledge, but the mouth of fools feeds on folly" (15:14).

One who is *intelligent*, who will attain to wisdom, will not wait for knowledge to come to him. He will *seek knowledge*. We often talk about wisdom coming through experience. This is true, but it does not come by experience *alone*. We must seek after knowledge that has been revealed from God and not be like the fool who is content with *folly*.

Related passages: Proverbs 18:15; 21:12.

Having the desire to learn is essential. But some may wonder if they will actually be able to obtain wisdom or if the pursuit of wisdom will be an exercise of futility. While the pursuit of *worldly* wisdom is futile (Ecclesiastes 1:17-18; 2:12-17), we are assured that we *will* be able to learn and gain *divine* wisdom.

> *"For the Lord gives wisdom; from His mouth come knowledge and understanding. He stores up sound wisdom for the upright; He is a shield to those who walk in integrity, guarding the paths of justice, and He preserves the way of His godly ones. Then you will discern righteousness and justice and equity and every good course. For wisdom will enter your heart and knowledge will be pleasant to your soul"* (2:6-10).

The wisdom that we are considering is the wisdom that comes from above. Because it is from Almighty God, it is able to be distributed according to His will without hindrance. James later wrote, *"But if any of you lacks wisdom, let him ask of God, who gives to all generously and without reproach, and it will be given to him"* (James 1:5). This prayer that James mentioned is not answered miraculously as it was with Solomon (1 Kings 3:5-12). Instead, it is answered as we follow the divinely prescribed way of obtaining wisdom, as the book of Proverbs discusses – through learning and practice of God's word. When we follow God's way of obtaining wisdom, we can be assured that we *will* grow in knowledge and acquire wisdom. Solomon says, *"You will discern,"* and, *"Wisdom will enter your heart."* Wisdom says, *"I love those who love me; and those who diligently seek me will find me"* (8:17).

Related passages: Proverbs 9:9; 14:18, 33.

However, though there is a promise that we *will* learn if we seek to learn, the book of Proverbs also teaches us that there are some who *will not learn*. Let us notice the reasons for this.

*"A scoffer seeks wisdom and finds none, but knowledge is easy to
one who has understanding"* (14:6).

This verse talks about one who *"seeks wisdom"* but *"finds none."* Though we
have already noticed how the *desire to learn* is essential (15:14; 18:15), the desire alone is not enough. One may claim to desire wisdom, and will therefore
seek after it; but if he is a *"scoffer,"* he will have no regard for the instruction
that would lead him to acquire wisdom. Therefore, though he seeks for it in
some sense, he will not obtain wisdom.

*"Like legs which are useless to the lame, so is a proverb in the
mouth of fools"* (26:7).

*"Like a thorn which falls into the hand of a drunkard, so is a
proverb in the mouth of fools"* (26:9).

The proverb delivered by the wise counselor is able to help the one who has
understanding. However, the fool, though he may know the proverb even to
the point of being able to repeat it, will not get any benefit from it. It is not that
he does not *know* it (it is in his mouth; he is able to speak it); it is that he does
not *understand* it and cannot *apply* it properly. To him, the proverb is as legs to
a lame man. Though he has them, he cannot use them properly, if at all. As he
seeks wisdom, which is pleasant like a rose, he comes away without the rose,
but with only the thorn stuck in his hand. Because he lacks understanding, he
will not acquire wisdom; and the vain pursuit of it will only bring harm to
himself.

Related passages: Proverbs 10:14; 14:8.

To Acquire Wisdom, We Must Be Humble

Humility is necessary in order to *acquire* wisdom. *"When pride comes, then* comes dishonor, but with the humble is wisdom" (11:2). As wisdom comes from instruction and understanding, we must be humble enough to admit our own lack of wisdom and the need to pursue it. Without humility, we will not believe we need wisdom and will, therefore, ignore it.

> "Trust in the Lord with all your heart and do not lean on your own understanding. In all your ways acknowledge Him, and He will make your paths straight. Do not be wise in your own eyes; fear the Lord and turn away from evil" (3:5-7).

When we possess *humility*, we will understand that there are answers we do not have and guidance that we need. Therefore, we will not "*lean on* [our] *own understanding*" or "*be wise in* [our] *own eyes.*" We will seek guidance and be open to instruction. However, it is important that we get the right guidance. So Solomon says we must put our trust *in the Lord*. Many today put their trust in parents, professors, or preachers to lead them in the paths of wisdom. While we may certainly be helped by the instruction of others (11:14; 15:22; 24:6), it is only when such instruction is in harmony with the wisdom that comes from above that it will do us any good. Therefore, our trust is not in others who might teach us but in the Lord.

Related passages: Proverbs 15:33; 28:13; 30:2-5.

As *humility* leads to wisdom and honor, *pride* leads to destruction.

> "Pride goes before destruction, and a haughty spirit before stumbling. It is better to be humble in spirit with the lowly than to divide the spoil with the proud" (16:18-19).

Pride leads to one's downfall. Elsewhere, Solomon adds to this thought: "*But humility goes before honor*" (18:12; cf. 29:23). This is why he says, "*It is better to be humble in spirit with the lowly.*" In the long term, it is better to be humble in order to later be exalted (cf. 1 Peter 5:5-6). However, most people tend to be shortsighted and look at the immediate *"spoil"* that is associated with *"the proud."* So they arrogantly follow the path of instant gratification. Yet in the end, as they have rejected divine wisdom, they will stumble and ultimately be destroyed.

> *"There is a way which seems right to a man, but its end is the way of death"* (14:12).

The one who is puffed up with pride trusts in his own way. He rejects instruction because he does not believe that he needs it. He is unwilling to change his thinking or his direction. Jeremiah said, *"I know, O Lord, that a man's way is not in himself, nor is it in a man who walks to direct his steps"* (Jeremiah 10:23). This is true for all men of all time. Without learning of God and His ways, we cannot find the way of life. When we reject the wisdom that comes from above, no matter what other direction we take, we will be on a path that leads to *death* (cf. 16:25).

> *"Do you see a man wise in his own eyes? There is more hope for a fool than for him"* (26:12).

The one who is *"wise in his own eyes"* is the one who has rejected divine wisdom for the *"way which seems right"* to him (14:12; 16:25). He is contrasted with the *fool* in this passage. Therefore, we must understand the *"fool"* of this verse to be one who simply *lacks* wisdom, not one who has *rejected* wisdom. Because he only *lacks* wisdom, there is *hope* for him that if he can receive the right instruction, he can acquire wisdom. However, for one who is *"wise in his own eyes,"* in his arrogance he sees no need to listen, learn, or acquire godly wisdom, even though his deficiency of wisdom will be apparent to others. Solomon offers two examples to illustrate this point. *"The sluggard is wiser in his own eyes than seven men who can give a discreet answer"* (26:16). Though the impoverished and miserable condition of the sluggard is apparent to those who know him, in his arrogance he cannot see the need to change anything about his life. *"The rich man is wise in his own eyes, but the poor who has un-*

derstanding sees through him" (28:11). The rich man of this verse is not a righteous man who happens to be blessed with riches. He is a rich man who puts
his trust in riches. This rich man may believe that he is fully self-sufficient and
that his prosperity is a sign that he has more than enough wisdom on his own
and needs no wisdom from God. Yet the poor man who has understanding
(divine wisdom) will be able to see the folly of the rich man's arrogance.

Related passage: Proverbs 30:12-13.

To Acquire Wisdom, We Must Be Disciplined

A willingness to listen, desire to learn, and spirit of humility are essential
for one to be able to *acquire* wisdom. But there is one more component that is
necessary – *discipline*. The instruction which we *listen to, learn,* and receive in
humility will get us on the path of wisdom. *Discipline* keeps us on the right
path once we are on it. If we ever stray from the path, *discipline* is what gets us
back on track. So the wise man says, "*Apply your heart to discipline and your
ears to words of knowledge*" (23:12).

> "*My son, do not reject the discipline of the Lord or loathe His re-
> proof, for whom the Lord loves He reproves, even as a father cor-
> rects the son in whom he delights*" (3:11-12).

Discipline is not pleasant when it is being administered. The discipline of
the Lord often comes to us today in the form of rebuke and correction from
His word and the negative consequences that come as a result of our disobedi-
ence. We are not to *reject* or *loathe* it. The reason why the Lord disciplines us is
not because He *hates* us, but because He *loves* us and wants to guide us to the
way that is right. The Hebrew writer explained this passage when he discussed
the suffering those brethren were experiencing at the hands of wicked men
(Hebrews 12:5-10). We are disciplined because we have a loving Father in
heaven who is committed to raising us properly. The Hebrew writer added: "*All*

discipline for the moment seems not to be joyful, but sorrowful; yet to those who have been trained by it, afterwards it yields the peaceful fruit of righteousness" (Hebrews 12:11). Ultimately, this discipline is for our good, even though it may not seem to be from a short-sighted perspective. This is why Solomon says elsewhere, *"A wise son accepts his father's discipline, but a scoffer does not listen to rebuke"* (13:1).

Related passages: Proverbs 15:32; 29:19.

Though discipline is necessary for one to learn, many do not see the point of trying to learn. The book of Proverbs contains a few passages that deal with the *benefit* of discipline and the end result of it.

> *"Listen to counsel and accept discipline, that you may be wise the*
> *rest of your days"* (19:20).

The New American Standard translates the second part of this verse, *"that you may be wise the rest of your days."* The King James Version is slightly different: *"That thou mayest be wise in thy latter end."* The former emphasizes a progression of gaining wisdom while the latter emphasizes the goal of possessing wisdom in the end. In either case, discipline is about our *future*, rather than the present. In the future, the discipline that leads us to grow in knowledge from God will result in wisdom, understanding, and honor (12:1; 13:18).

> *"For the commandment is a lamp and the teaching is light; and*
> *reproofs for discipline are the way of life"* (6:23).

In the previous verses, we saw that *discipline* leads to wisdom (19:20), understanding (12:1), and honor (13:18). If these were not enough to convince one of the benefits of discipline, the wise man adds here that the path of discipline is *"the way of life."* It will help us avoid trouble in this life (6:24-35), as well as in the next (7:22-27).

Related passages: Proverbs 15:5; 20:30.

Unfortunately, not all are willing to accept discipline as being for their good. Some will reject it. This has consequences.

> *"Grievous punishment is for him who forsakes the way; he who hates reproof will die"* (15:10).

The way that is being forsaken is the way of *wisdom*. Those who reject God's standard and do not walk according to it will be punished. The goal of discipline ("*reproof*") is correction so that the one who once rejected God's ways will return to them. One who "*hates reproof*" will continue on the path that leads away from life and, without an appropriate change of direction, will eventually face *death* – not physical death (which we must all face) but eternal separation from God.

Related passages: Proverbs 19:27; 26:3; 29:1.

* * *

The passages we have noticed so far on the topic of *discipline* have had to do with *receiving* discipline. But what if we are the ones needing to exercise discipline and reprove others? The book of Proverbs contains instructions that teach us how we are to administer discipline and warns us of how it will often be received.

> *"He who corrects a scoffer gets dishonor for himself, and he who reproves a wicked man gets insults for himself. Do not reprove a scoffer, or he will hate you, reprove a wise man and he will love you"* (9:7-8).

The dishonor one receives when he corrects a scoffer is from the scoffer himself. He is not interested in learning the way of wisdom. He simply wants to do what seems right to him. Therefore, if one tries to correct him, *"he will hate you."* Elsewhere it says, *"A scoffer does not love one who reproves him, he will not go to the wise"* (15:12). Rather than responding with gratitude, as the wise man will, the scoffer will respond with *insults* directed toward the one attempting to correct him. One must have a thick skin if he is going to correct others, or else he will soon abandon his attempts.

Related passages: Proverbs 16:22; 17:10; 27:22.

> *"Strike a scoffer and the naive may become shrewd, but reprove one who has understanding and he will gain knowledge"* (19:25).

From the earlier passages, it may seem as though the discipline of fools is pointless. If they will not listen and correct their ways, why bother trying to correct them at all? The answer is found in this verse. When a person *"strike*[s] *a scoffer,"* though one may be dishonored, insulted, and hated (9:7-8), others may be helped by one's efforts. Though the scoffer may not change, *"the naive"* who witness your efforts may learn the lesson that was intended for the one receiving the discipline. As a result, he may become *shrewd* or *wise* (cf. 21:11).

> *"He who rebukes a man will afterward find more favor than he who flatters with the tongue"* (28:23).

This is another passage that reminds us that it is better to try to correct someone than not, even if we risk the insults and hatred that sometimes come from one who rejects discipline. Flattering the one who needs to change does nothing to help them. Rebuking him may result in insults and hatred (9:7-8). Or it could lead him to *"love you"* (9:8) as he learns the way of wisdom. *"Better is open rebuke than love that is concealed"* (27:5). Better to rebuke someone on the chance that he will repent than to flatter him and thus provide implicit encouragement for him to remain in his sin.

Questions on Lesson 3

1. What is the beginning of wisdom (9:10)? Why?

2. Why is listening necessary for one to obtain wisdom?

3. What does 9:9 say about the ongoing process of acquiring wisdom?

4. Why does the scoffer not find wisdom when he seeks for it (14:6)?

5. Why did Agur say he was *more stupid than any man* (30:2)?

6. Why does the Lord reprove His people (3:11-12; cf. Hebrews 12:5-11)?

7. Though reproving a scoffer may seem futile (9:7-8), why is it still necessary (19:25)?

The Application of Wisdom

It is absolutely essential that we recognize the *appeal* of wisdom. Once we know that Wisdom is calling to us, we must learn to *appreciate* wisdom so that we have a reason to pay attention to her appeals. Understanding this, we then need to work toward *acquiring* wisdom. But all of this is futile if, after we do all to *acquire* it, we do not *apply* wisdom.

The bulk of the book of Proverbs, and the majority of our study, focuses on the *application* of wisdom. When God reveals His wisdom, man is not to pursue it merely out of intellectual curiosity. God expects us to put what we learn into practice.

> *"Every prudent man acts with knowledge, but a fool displays folly"* (13:16).

A *"prudent man"* does not merely *possess* knowledge, though he certainly does possess it. He will do more than just *acquire* knowledge. He will *act with knowledge.* The things that he learns will be put on display in his life, just as folly is on display in the life of the fool.

> *"Doing wickedness is like sport to a fool, and so is wisdom to a man of understanding"* (10:23).

The fool is said to *enjoy* practicing wickedness. It is like a sport to him. A contrast is made between the fool and the man of understanding. The fool enjoys *"doing wickedness."* Though *"doing"* is not explicitly stated in regard to wisdom, the contrast implies it. Just as the fool enjoys *"doing wickedness,"* the man of understanding enjoys *doing* that which is wise.

"A plan in the heart of a man is like deep water, but a man of understanding draws it out" (20:5).

Water that is at the bottom of a deep well has the *potential* to do good, but only when one does what is necessary to draw it out is it actually helpful to him. In the same way, having plans and intentions to do good and act with wisdom only have the *potential* of doing good. One who has learned the truth has the capacity to act with wisdom. But he must draw it out of his heart (mind) so that it is manifested in his actions. Only then will wisdom actually benefit the one who possesses it.

"Like a dog returns to its vomit is a fool who repeats his folly" (26:11).

One who will repeatedly go back to his sin and walk in foolishness is like the dog with its ignorant and disgusting behavior. There is no benefit for returning to one's foolish ways. If one had sense, he would be repulsed by the thought of returning to his folly. But the fool, like the dog who returns to its vomit, keeps going back to his sin. The instructions given in the book of Proverbs are not just for us to learn what is expected of us. They are written so that we might forsake our sin and follow after righteousness.

So as we seek to *apply* wisdom, there are several topics which we will discuss as we move through our study. We will not cover every in the book of Proverbs in our study. But we will examine the major topics as we learn more about the *application* of wisdom.

Lesson 4

The Application: Character

Key verses: Proverbs 6:16-19; 14:29-30; 20:6; 22:1; 30:15-16

As one learns to accept the wisdom that comes from above, the result will be a change of character. As we consider some of the character traits that one will gain from a pursuit of wisdom, let us first begin by contrasting them with the negative character traits of one who rejects divine wisdom. Below is a list the wise man gives of seven abominations.

Seven Abominations

Read: Proverbs 6:16-19

Haughty eyes are an abomination to the Lord. Therefore, the wise man will be humble. The wise man is clear in connecting pride with sin. "*Haughty eyes and a proud heart, the lamp of the wicked, is sin*" (21:4; cf. 21:24). Pride causes one to seek to elevate self, while the Scriptures teach that we should be humble enough that any praise we receive is not from ourselves, but from others. "*Let another praise you, and not your own mouth; a stranger, and not your own lips*" (27:2). Pride also blinds one to his own sins. "*Who can say, 'I have cleansed my heart, I am pure from my sin'?*" (20:9). All men have sinned (Romans 3:23) and are in need of repentance. Those who deny this, in their arrogance, deceive themselves (1 John 1:8). Therefore, we must be humble if we are to follow the ways of wisdom.

A lying tongue is an abomination to the Lord. Therefore, the wise man will be honest. Solomon says elsewhere, "*Lying lips are an abomination to the Lord, but those who deal faithfully are His delight*" (12:22). As lying is an abomination to the Lord, the *"righteous man* [also] *hates falsehood"* (13:5). One who is following after God's wisdom will not be like many in the world who are truthful when it is convenient but are more than willing to compromise their integrity in order to enrich themselves. The wise man says, *"It is better to be a poor man than a liar"* (19:22).

Hands that shed innocent blood are an abomination to the Lord. Therefore, the wise man will be merciful. Solomon says, *"A man's discretion makes him slow to anger, and it is his glory to overlook a transgression"* (19:11). This verse is not about one condoning or tolerating sin, but rather that the wise man will desire a sinner's repentance and be willing to forgive. Even when it comes to one's enemies, though *"men of bloodshed hate the blameless...the upright are concerned for his life"* (29:10). The trait of mercy ought to become so ingrained into one's character that he will not only be merciful to his fellow man, but will even have *"regard for the life of his animal"* (12:10).

A heart that devises wicked plans is an abomination to the Lord. Therefore, the wise man will keep his thoughts pure. A man's character is rooted in his heart. *"As in water face reflects face, so the heart of man reflects man"* (27:19). From the heart *"flow the springs of life"* (4:23). Therefore, the wise man will guard his heart from wickedness. Solomon says, *"The desire of the righteous is only good, but the expectation of the wicked is wrath"* (11:23).

Feet that run rapidly to evil are an abomination to the Lord. Therefore, the wise man will seek to do good. There are two problems with the wicked man here – his direction (toward evil) and his carelessness (he runs rapidly). In regard to direction, Solomon says, *"The way of a guilty man is crooked, but as for the pure, his conduct is upright"* (21:8). Elsewhere he says, *"A man of understanding walks straight"* (15:21), and, *"The highway of the upright is to depart from evil; he who watches his way preserves life"* (16:17). The wise man later says, *"Better is the poor man who walks in his integrity than he who is crooked though he be rich"* (28:6; cf. 19:1). But besides going the wrong direction, the wicked man is also careless. In contrast, the wise man will be careful and will consider how he walks. "*A wise man is cautious and turns away from evil, but a fool is arrogant and careless. A quick-tempered man acts foolishly...*" (14:16-17). The one who is in control of his emotions, however, will act with wisdom.

A *false witness* is an abomination to the Lord. Therefore, the wise man will be just and fair. Earlier in the list was the abomination of a lying tongue. A false witness is different even though they both involve dishonesty. The false witness does not just utter a falsehood, but is offering false testimony against another, thereby denying that person justice. Solomon says, "*The thoughts of the righteous are just, but the counsels of the wicked are deceitful*" (12:5). We should heed the warning: "*A false witness will not go unpunished, and he who tells lies will not escape*" (19:5). Since we will be held accountable, wisdom demands that we be fair and just in our treatment of others.

One who spreads strife is an abomination to the Lord. Therefore, the wise man will seek peace. There are a few warnings in the book of Proverbs that describe the destructiveness of strife. "*A stone is heavy and the sand weighty, but the provocation of a fool is heavier than both of them. Wrath is fierce and anger is a flood, but who can stand before jealousy?*" (27:3-4). "*An angry man stirs up strife, and a hot-tempered man abounds in transgression*" (29:22). "*Scorners set a city aflame, but wise men turn away anger*" (29:8). The strife that is caused by an angry man is like a crushing rock and a fire that burns down a city. But the last verse above describes the peacemaking efforts of the wise man – "*wise men turn away anger.*" Though peace is not always possible, Paul later said, "*So far as it depends on you, be at peace with all men*" (Romans 12:18). One who pursues divine wisdom will seek peace whenever it is possible.

* * *

In addition to the lessons we can learn from the seven abominations, there are other character traits that one will gain from his pursuit of the wisdom that comes from above.

Self-Control

One who pursues wisdom will learn to exercise control over his emotions, rather than being controlled by them.

Read: Proverbs 14:29-30

All men, no matter if they are wise or foolish, will encounter circumstances in their lives that could lead them to become angry. The difference is that the wise man will have control over his emotions so that he is not quick to become angry. The man without self-control will react quickly, thereby increasing folly. Solomon says elsewhere, "*A fool's anger is known at once, but a prudent man conceals dishonor*" (12:16). "*He who restrains his words has knowledge, and he who has a cool spirit is a man of understanding*" (17:27). "*A fool always loses his temper, but a wise man holds it back*" (29:11). Though the contrast between the wise and foolish is clear, it does take effort to exercise self-control. The wise man also says, "*He who is slow to anger is better than the mighty, and he who rules his spirit, than he who captures a city*" (16:32). He presents the picture of a celebrated military commander or warrior who is able to capture a city. The ability to be able to do this commands respect. However, the wise man says that one who is able to control his emotions ("*rules his spirit*") is more accomplished than the warrior, thus showing the great discipline and effort necessary for one to exercise self-control.

Related passages: Proverbs 25:16, 27-28.

Trustworthiness

As one follows the wisdom that comes from above, he will also prove himself to be *trustworthy*.

Read: Proverbs 20:6

Many are quick to claim that they are trustworthy and reliable. Yet how many actually are? According to the wise man, the number who are trustworthy is far less than those who claim to be. Man in general, as he rejects the wisdom that comes from above, will not be trustworthy. Why? It is because he has no greater standard than himself. He may keep his word when it is advantageous for him to do so. But when it seems better for him to go back on his word, he does it. The implication is that the one following divine wisdom will be trustworthy because he values *honesty* and works to build a good *reputation*.

Related passages: Proverbs 25:19; 26:6.

Reputation

Wisdom also leads one to develop a *good reputation* among his brethren.

Read: Proverbs 22:1

The wise man reminds us how valuable a good reputation can be. Silver and gold can be obtained, even by wicked men. This wealth can also be lost through no fault of the one who possesses it. Yet one's "*good name*" cannot be lost as long as he maintains it. This "*good name*" comes as the result of consistently doing good and following after the wisdom that comes from above. Nothing that is of this world (even silver and gold) can compare with that. We must be sure our priorities are in order and work on establishing a good reputation based upon good works, rather than placing our focus on obtaining the perishable wealth of this world.

Related passages: Proverbs 20:6, 11; 27:21.

Contentment

Following after the wisdom that comes from above, as it helps one to realize what is truly important, will lead to *contentment*.

Read: Proverbs 30:15-16

These verses further describe the insatiable desire of the fool by comparing it to various other things that will never be content. The leech's two daughters constantly cry for more. Sheol is the grave. It is always open to more lost souls who would enter into it. The barren womb is never satisfied, as God made it for the purpose of bringing forth children. When no children are brought forth, there is no contentment there. The earth will always receive the rain that falls upon it. The fire will never stop burning as long as there is fuel for it. The fool, like all of these that are never satisfied, cannot be content, no matter how much he acquires of this world's goods. As we follow after God's wisdom, we will naturally learn contentment because we will come to understand that all the things that the fool desires are only temporary. As Solomon says later, "*Do not weary yourself to gain wealth, cease from your consideration of it. When you set your eyes on it, it is gone*" (23:4-5). Let us learn contentment, rather than waste our lives in the endless pursuit of material things.

Related passages: Proverbs 27:7-8, 20.

Questions on Lesson 4

1. What seven things are listed as being abominations to the Lord (6:16-19)?

2. What advice is given to one who has *"found honey"* (25:16)? What larger principle does this illustrate?

3. In what way is a city without walls like a man without self-control (25:28)?

4. By what means does one distinguish himself (20:11)?

5. Why is a "*good name...to be more desired than great wealth*" (22:1)?

6. Why does the "*sated man*" loathe honey (27:7)?

7. What are the four things that "*will not be satisfied*" (30:15-16)?

Lesson 5

The Application: Speech

Key verses: Proverbs 17:7; 25:11; 12:13; 18:21; 10:21; 11:9; 12:17-19; 17:27-28

The next area of *application* has to do with our *speech*. Exercising wisdom is not just about what we *do* but also includes those things which we *speak*.

Read: Proverbs 17:7

A fool will not appreciate wisdom, listen to wisdom, or grow in wisdom. This will be seen in his character (as has already been discussed) and in his *words*. One who fails to acquire wisdom will not speak the words of wisdom. The wise man, however, as he grows in wisdom will develop *"excellent speech,"* which will then be evident to all who hear him.

The Value of Good Words

Earlier in the study we considered the *value of wisdom* and how it is worth far more than gold, silver, and other valuable things of this life. As wisdom produces *"excellent speech"* (17:7), we would expect that the words spoken by one who has acquired wisdom would also be valuable. Various passages in the book of Proverbs show this to be the case.

Read: Proverbs 10:11

Good words lead to life. This can refer to the fact that one who keeps his speech upright will be blessed in this life. It is also true that one who speaks the words of righteousness contributes to the spiritual well-being of himself and all who hear him. In contrast, the speech of the wicked *"conceals violence,"* hiding the harm that comes from his destructive speech.

Read: Proverbs 25:11, 25

The two verses above describe the great value of words of *encouragement*. The word picture of *"apples of gold in settings of silver"* is a symbol of the beauty and richness of words that are used to build up others. The *"cold water to a weary soul"* is used to describe encouraging words as being refreshing and even life-saving. Without good words to encourage and provide instruction of the ways of God, there is no reason for hope and no path to life.

Related passages: Proverbs 10:20, 31-32; 20:15; 15:26

The Consequences of Evil Words

Besides the fact that good words are valuable, using proper speech is also important because of the negative consequences that come from evil words.

Read: Proverbs 12:13

An evil man is going to speak things that are also evil. Remember: *"For as he thinks within himself, so he is"* (23:7). His evil thoughts are going to come out in the words he uses. When this happens and he sins with his lips, he will bring trouble upon himself. The wise man says elsewhere, *"In the mouth of the foolish is a rod for his back, but the lips of the wise will protect them"* (14:3). The good words of the wise man will provide protection from harm that might otherwise come against him. In contrast, the evil words of the foolish man will only endanger him.

Read: Proverbs 20:17

It is common for people to lie in order to get what they want. When they do this, they may have the initial satisfaction and pleasure of enjoying whatever it is that they were able to obtain through falsehood. But this *"sweet"* taste will eventually change, as if *"his mouth* [were] *filled with gravel."* This could possibly refer to the guilt that one may later have for lying in order to acquire what he wants. It can also refer to the negative consequences of lying – such as receiving the bad reputation of being a liar or the threat of vengeance from the one who was deceived. Either way, Solomon is emphasizing the fact that lying in order to gain some sort of advantage is common, but it is neither wise nor beneficial in the long term.

Related passages: Proverbs 20:19-20; 30:32-33

The Power of Words

We sometimes hear the saying, "The pen is mightier than the sword." This concept of *words* being more powerful than physical force is similar to the idea expressed by Solomon: *"Death and life are in the power of the tongue"* (18:21). Words are powerful. The wise man shows us the power of both good and evil words.

Read: Proverbs 10:21

The words of the righteous do not only provide a benefit to themselves but are able to help others as well. In this verse, Solomon says their words *"feed many."* In our society, many people have the idea that to *"feed many"* requires great amounts of money and expansive government programs. Yet Solomon says *"the lips of the righteous"* are able to do this. How could such words help *feed* others? They impart words of wisdom that will help others to be more productive and self-sufficient, relying upon the blessings that God has given rather than being in need. Later in this study we will consider the Proverbs about *work* and *stewardship*. Teaching others in such ways of wisdom will help *"feed many."*

Related passages: Proverbs 12:25; 25:15

As good words are powerful, so also are evil words.

Read: Proverbs 11:9

We might expect that the godless man, by his evil words, would be able to annoy, anger, or inconvenience his neighbor. But Solomon says that the evil words of the godless man are able to *destroy* his neighbor. Through lies, deception, slander, wicked counsel, and false testimony, one is able to ruin the life, and even jeopardize the soul, of another.

Related passages: Proverbs 16:27-28; 27:3; 26:20-28

Other Proverbs About Speech

As we noticed in the previous section, we should never underestimate the *power of words* – both good and evil. Understanding how important our speech is, we must be sure that our words reflect *wisdom* at all times.

Speaking Truth or Lies – One area in which there will be a sharp contrast between the wise man and the fool is that the one who follows after God's wisdom will speak *truth*. The one who rejects divine wisdom (which is truth in itself) will speak what is *false*.

Read: Proverbs 12:17-19

The wise man mentions a couple of the benefits that come from speaking the truth. First, speaking truth imparts "*what is right*" (12:17) or "*righteousness*" (KJV). Second, speaking truth "*brings healing*" (12:18). Third, there is a long-term benefit for those who speak truth in that they will be "*established forever*" (12:19). This is in contrast with the one who speaks lies.

Solomon says, "*A lying tongue is only for a moment*" (12:19). Speaking lies leads to punishment; as the wise man says elsewhere: "*A false witness will not go unpunished, and he who tells lies will perish*" (19:9). Speaking falsehood will not only cause trouble in this life; it causes trouble beyond this life. So Solomon says, "*He who guards his mouth and his tongue, guards his soul from troubles*" (21:23). We must work to control our tongues so that we do not get ourselves into trouble, either in this life or in the next.

Related passages: Proverbs 12:22; 4:24; 14:5, 25; 25:14

Carefulness and Discretion – We sometimes hear the phrase, "think before you speak." This principle is found in the book of Proverbs. Solomon encourages us to exercise carefulness and discretion in our speech.

Read: Proverbs 17:27-28

Carefulness and discretion in speech is so clearly a characteristic of wisdom that Solomon says that a fool who restrains his words and "*keeps silent, is considered wise*" (17:28). The reason why refraining from unnecessary speech is a characteristic of wisdom is because the more one speaks, the more trouble can be caused by his speech. The wise man even goes so far as to say, "*When there are many words, transgression is unavoidable*" (10:19). One who does not learn to control his tongue can expect to sin with his tongue. James said the tongue was "*a restless evil and full of deadly poison*" (James 3:8). Therefore, we must take great care to restrain our words and only speak things which are good and right.

Related passages: Proverbs 10:10, 13-14; 12:23; 11:12-13; 17:9; 18:13; 20:25; 13:3; 29:20

Teaching – One of the important things we can do in our speech is *teaching*. Solomon discusses this in the book of Proverbs as well.

Read: Proverbs 15:7

The wisdom that comes from above is not intended for an elite few while others are left without it. If we have acquired knowledge, we should want to share what we know so that others can also gain knowledge and become wise. It is the mark of a fool for one to not want to spread knowledge and help others learn what they ought to know.

Read: Proverbs 24:24-26

The prophet Isaiah said, "*Woe to those who call evil good, and good evil*" (Isaiah 5:20). Though there is often a tendency today for men to praise those who do what is wrong, we help no one when we call the wicked righteous. We must be willing to call sin for what it is. We should *rebuke* wickedness, not praise or excuse it. If we rebuke wickedness we will be blessed. If we fail to do this, and praise the wicked instead, we will be cursed.

Related passages: Proverbs 24:24-26; 26:4-5; 17:4; 28:10

Questions on Lesson 5

1. What happens to a man after he obtains bread by falsehood (20:17)? Why?

2. Why should one "*not associate with a gossip*" (20:19)?

3. How are the "*lips of the righteous*" able to "*feed many*" (10:21)?

4. How is a godless man's speech able to destroy his neighbor (11:9)?

5. How is a man who falsely boasts of his gifts like clouds and wind with no rain (25:14)?

6. Why should one not quickly claim something to be holy (20:25)?

7. At first glance, the instructions in 26:4-5 about answering a fool may seem like a contradiction. Explain the meaning of the passage.

Lesson 6

The Application: Work

Key verses: Proverbs 14:23; 16:26; 15:19; 28:19; 13:4; 6:6-11

When we consider the subject of *work*, Solomon's words in Ecclesiastes provide a fitting starting point: "*Whatever your hand finds to do, do it with all your might; for there is no activity or planning or knowledge or wisdom in Sheol where you are going*" (Ecclesiastes 9:10). Our time here on earth is limited. Therefore, we must work hard in the time that we have. Once our lives here are over, there will be no opportunity to do what we ought to have done during our time under the sun. So the wise man spends a good deal of time in the book of Proverbs discussing the important topic of work.

The Virtue and Rewards of Work

We learn in Solomon's writings that work is not only necessary and honorable but that it also leads to blessings from God as we carry out the responsibilities we have in life.

Read: Proverbs 14:23

Some seem to have the idea that some work is worthwhile, but other work is useless. It is certainly true that from a financial standpoint, certain types of labor are more profitable than others. But Solomon says that "*all labor*" is profitable. He then warns us against spending all of our time merely talking and planning about what we might do. It is easy to become so distracted by plans and dreams that we do not accomplish any actual work. No matter how good our plans or how ambitious our dreams are, they are worthless if we never do any work to make those plans a reality.

Read: Proverbs 16:26

When God created man, he gave him a natural indicator in his own body that would remind him of the need to eat to sustain his life – hunger. Solomon says this hunger motivates man to work hard so that he can sustain himself from the fruit of his labors. One of the reasons many become trapped in the rut of laziness is because they do not feel the motivation of hunger to urge them to work hard. When laziness is rewarded or subsidized, people will continue in laziness. When laziness causes one to be hungry, people will eventually learn that they must work so that they will be able to eat. Later in the book of Proverbs, Agur mentions three things which cause the earth to quake and four under which it "*cannot bear up*" (30:21). One of these is "*a fool when he is satisfied with food*" (30:22). When one refuses to work and suffers hunger because of it, he harms himself. When one refuses to work but is rewarded for his laziness with food and the necessities of life, society is harmed because of it.

Related passages: Proverbs 20:29; 21:5; 28:20; 22:29; 12:24

The Consequences of Refusing to Work

The wise man warns us that there are consequences for refusing to work. These consequences go beyond simply missing out on the blessings of hard work. There are also negative consequences that come for those who refuse to work.

Read: Proverbs 15:19

There are two paths one can take in life – "*the way of the lazy*" and "*the path of the upright*." In context, the *upright* is one who is a diligent worker. One who is lazy tries to avoid the hard work in which the diligent man engages. Yet this verse mentions the difficulties and come from laziness. The path of the diligent man is a *highway* – clear and easy to travel. The path of the lazy man goes through a *hedge of thorns*. The point is that everything is more difficult for one who does not develop the ability or possess the inclination to work hard.

Read: Proverbs 28:19

We noticed earlier that *"the plans of the diligent lead surely to advantage"* (21:5). The path to prosperity is not short, but takes time and requires one to follow certain procedures – in this case, tilling his land so that he might later reap the harvest. Solomon says, *"The sluggard does not plow after the autumn, so he begs during the harvest and has nothing"* (20:4). Even if one realizes his mistake late in the year, it will be too late. He cannot begin planting when it is time to be harvesting. Often when one does not do what needs to be done in the proper time, he will suffer for it. *"Laziness casts into a deep sleep, and an idle man will suffer hunger"* (19:15).

Related passages: Proverbs 18:9; 24:30-34

The Description of the Sluggard

In order to provide motivation for one to *work*, Solomon describes the conditions of the sluggard so that we might avoid being like him.

Read: Proverbs 13:4

Everyone has desires they wish to be fulfilled – from the basic necessities of life (the desire for food, clothing, and shelter), to various comforts and luxuries of life. One who is diligent has a way to obtain what he desires – *work*. The sluggard, because he is not willing to work, *"craves and gets nothing."* Solomon later says, *"The desire of the sluggard puts him to death, for his hands refuse to work; all day long he is craving, while the righteous gives and does not hold back"* (21:25-26). The righteous man is able to be generous because of the reward he receives from his diligent labor (cf. Ephesians 4:28). The sluggard, because of his refusal to work, will not only have to live without certain things, but his laziness actually helps bring destruction upon himself.

Read: Proverbs 26:13

This verse is simply about one making excuses in an attempt to justify his laziness. A similar passages reads: "*The sluggard says, 'There is a lion outside; I will be killed in the streets!'*" (22:13). The sluggard uses the presence of a dangerous lion outside (assuming this was not a contrived excuse) to justify his remaining at home, in bed (26:14), not taking care of himself (26:15), and all the while thinking that he is "*wiser...than seven men who can give a discreet answer*" (26:16). Yet the sluggard is not wise for refusing to go out and work to provide for himself – even with a lion outside. If there was an actual lion outside, the sluggard could have done one of two things: either *kill* the lion or *avoid* the lion. But he refused to do either one. Too often people tend to make excuses to try and justify their laziness rather than simply deal with the problems and obstacles in front of them. The sluggard is the one who makes excuses. The wise man will find a way to work around any obstacle that presents itself.

Related passages: Proverbs 12:27; 26:14-15; 19:24

Admonition to the Sluggard

After describing the sluggard and explaining some of the consequences for one's refusal to work, we turn our attention to Solomon's admonition to the sluggard.

Read: Proverbs 6:6-11

The sluggard can learn from observing the ant. First, the ant is *self-motivated*. Though it has "*no chief, officer or ruler,*" it accomplishes the work that is necessary for it to do. It does not need to wait to be told what is required of it. Second, the ant is *prepared for the future*. During the winter months there would be no food to be found. So the ant works hard during the summer and harvest in order to have food later in the year. Third, the ant *does not procrastinate*. In the summer months, the ant begins gathering for the winter. Yet the sluggard prefers sleep over work, and, as a result, neglects to do the work necessary to provide for himself. Because of this, he will find himself in poverty and being forced to beg (cf. 24:33-34; 20:4).

Read: Proverbs 20:13

Sleep is necessary. But work is necessary, too. In this context, one who *loves sleep* is not one who simply appreciates the benefits of sleep and understands the necessity of rest for helping him carry out the responsibilities that he has in life. Rather, the one who *loves sleep* is one who will *neglect* his responsibilities in order to sleep. For him, rest is not a way to recharge from work but a way to *avoid* work. If we want to be "*satisfied with food*," meaning we have sufficient means of providing for ourselves, we must not "*love sleep*" like the sluggard.

Related passages: Proverbs 30:24-28

Questions on Lesson 6

1. Why does Solomon say, *"In all labor there is profit"* (14:23)? Is this true in every situation?

2. According to 12:24, will the lazy man be able to avoid work forever?

3. If a man repents of his slothfulness, will he escape the consequences of that sin? Explain (see 28:19).

4. In what way is one who is slack in his work like one who destroys (18:9)?

5. What could the sluggard do about the lion instead of making excuses for not leaving the house (26:13; 22:13)?

6. Why should one not love sleep (20:13)? What does that mean?

7. What lesson is learned from the four small creatures in 30:24-28?

Lesson 7

The Application: Stewardship

Key verses: Proverbs 10:2, 4-5; 3:9-10; 13:22; 24:27; 30:8-9; 10:22; 11:4; 16:8; 19:4; 6:1-5; 22:7

Stewardship refers to how we use the money and possessions we have. The book of Proverbs contains instructions that help us know how to be wise stewards of those things which we have.

Obtaining Wealth

We begin our study of *stewardship* by noticing the wise man's counsel about how we obtain wealth in the first place.

Read: Proverbs 10:2, 4-5

"*Treasures*" that come as a result of "*wickedness*" (KJV) are not the type of possessions we should desire. It does matter how we obtain our wealth. Rather than seeking to become rich through *wickedness*, we are to practice *righteousness*. How does one acquire wealth in a righteous manner? He does so by being *diligent* and not putting off the responsibilities of life. Though many wish to do so, we cannot escape the need to work hard. Solomon says, "*He who tills his land will have plenty of bread, but he who pursues worthless things lacks sense*" (12:11). We should strive to gain prosperity through hard work, not through deception. "*Wealth obtained by fraud dwindles, but the one who gathers by labor increases it*" (13:11).

Read: Proverbs 20:21

We have likely all heard stories of individuals who have won millions of dollars in the lottery, only to be broke in just a few years. They became rich very quickly – just as many people would like to do. But that great windfall of wealth "*will not be blessed in the end.*" It will not last because the one who acquired it does not know how to handle it. Therefore, the wealth will be squandered and lost; and he will be back in the same condition in which he was at the beginning.

Related passages: Proverbs 15:27; 21:6; 28:8, 22; 20:14

The Wise Use of Wealth

After we obtain wealth, we need to use it wisely. There are several passages in the book of Proverbs that speak to this.

Read: Proverbs 3:9-10

The wise man reminds us that we are to be mindful of God when we consider how we use our wealth. Our service to God is to be our highest priority, as we honor Him "*from the first*" of our produce. We focus on pleasing the Lord first, then let everything else follow. However, we need to be careful not to interpret passages like this one as some sort of guarantee of material prosperity as the reward of faithfulness to God. Those who teach the "health and wealth" gospel will try to do this, promising people material prosperity for one's faith (which, according to these false teachers, is usually demonstrated by one sending money to their "ministry"). Even without the false guarantee of the "health and wealth" preachers, there are blessings for following the Lord. Our focus, however, must be primarily upon serving God and being good stewards of the blessings He has given.

Read: Proverbs 13:22

Three things are necessary for one to be able to leave an inheritance for his grandchildren. First, he must spend a lifetime in diligent labor. Second, he must be a good steward of the fruits of his labor so that he is able to save enough to have something to provide for his grandchildren as an inheritance. And third, he must have a desire to help them that is stronger than any desire to use the money on himself. Of course, it is possible for one to be a good man and, because of factors beyond his control, not have an inheritance to leave for his children, let alone his grandchildren. But regardless of the variables and possible outcomes, a good man will have these characteristics – diligence, frugalness, and generosity.

Related passages: Proverbs 10:15; 18:10-11; 13:7; 11:24-26

The Wise Use of Our Possessions

Being a good steward does not just pertain to one's wealth but also to one's possessions. Let us notice the passages in Proverbs that discuss how to make wise use of our possessions.

Read: Proverbs 24:27

This verse is about *time management* in making wise use of our possessions. Both preparing one's field and building one's house are necessary. But if one does not tend to his field at the appropriate time, he will have nothing during the time of harvest (cf. 20:4). Because of the patience required in allowing the natural processes in God's providence to work, certain matters are more pressing than others. If one fails to recognize this, the field that he possesses could become worthless to him.

Read: Proverbs 14:4

Solomon reminds us here of the value of practicality over aesthetics. Animals – such as oxen – are dirty, stinky creatures. There is also a lot of work and expense required to keep such animals. However, the reason why one would endure the unpleasantness, work, and expense of keeping these animals is because *"much revenue comes by the strength of the ox."* If we judged and kept our possessions on the basis of beauty and sentimentality alone, we would find ourselves in poverty. While such impractical things may be fine to a point, we do need to possess and maintain those things which are practical and can help us survive and prosper.

Related passages: Proverbs 12:10; 27:23-27

Our Attitude Toward Riches

According to the words of Agur, there is a balance which we must strike in our attitude toward riches.

Read: Proverbs 30:8-9

There is a danger in having an abundance of riches because it can lead us to deny the Lord, thinking that we are fully self-sufficient without Him. However, lacking riches to the point of being in need is also dangerous because it could lead us to steal. He encourages us to be *content* – not being overly desirous of riches, but also being mindful and thankful for what we do have. This contentment comes when we understand the truth about riches and have the right attitude about them.

* * *

The most fundamental truth we must understand about riches is that they are *blessings from God.*

Read: Proverbs 10:22

Everything that we have to enjoy in this life comes from God. Therefore, we should always be mindful that He is the source of our blessings, as this will help us to focus on serving Him. But Solomon adds to his statement about God's abundant blessings. Not only is it true that the good things that we have to enjoy in this life come from God, but also He adds *"no sorrow with it"* (KJV). People often want to attribute bad things in their lives to God, but the wise man reminds us that good things – and only good things – are from the Lord. Though He may allow certain bad things to happen, He is not actively bringing harm upon us.

Related passages: Proverbs 14:24

* * *

Although riches are *blessings from God*, there is a danger posed by them if we foolishly trust in them. So Solomon warns: *do not trust in riches*.

Read: Proverbs 11:4

Though there is certainly a benefit provided to one who has riches, there is a limit to their usefulness. In the *"day of wrath,"* or the day of divine judgment, our wealth will not save us. When it comes time to depart from this life, riches will not prevent our death, nor will we be able to take our possessions with us into the afterlife.

Related passages: Proverbs 11:28; 18:10-11; 23:4-5

* * *

Some place too much stock in riches. Others despise any form of wealth. We need to learn to place a *proper valuation on wealth*.

Read: Proverbs 12:9

In order to have a servant, one would need to first have a certain degree of wealth. Even though others may have little regard for him, it is better to have this wealth than not. Lacking bread is not honorable (this is different than *sacrificing*, which would be honorable). Therefore, the one who lacks bread will only receive honor from himself. So riches are valuable and should not be quickly disregarded.

Read: Proverbs 16:8

On the other hand, while riches are valuable, they are not more valuable than righteousness. If the only way to obtain wealth is by dealing unjustly with others, it is better to maintain one's integrity and live in humble circumstances. Righteousness before God will *always* be more important than the riches of this life.

* * *

In developing a proper attitude toward riches, it is important that we understand how our wealth influences others.

Read: Proverbs 14:20; 19:4

A sad reality in life is that many people value friendships based upon what they can get out of the relationship. If someone might be in a position to help them in the form of labor, connections, or material prosperity, many will be more friendly to such a person than to one who is not able to offer such things. This is Solomon's point. People want to be friends with the wealthy in the hopes of obtaining some financial benefit from the relationship. The poor cannot offer this, so they are despised and their friendship is disregarded. Solomon reinforces this point a couple verses after the second one listed above: "*Many will seek the favor of a generous man, and every man is a friend to him who gives gifts. All the brothers of a poor man hate him; how much more do his friends abandon him! He pursues them with words, but they are gone*" (19:6-7). Sadly, the benefit the poor man has to offer through his *words* (teaching, encouragement, etc.) is not worth nearly as much (in the eyes of many) as the "*gifts*" distributed by the wealthy to his friends.

Related passages: Proverbs 18:16; 21:14

Things to Avoid

As we are encouraged to be good stewards of the blessings we have received from God, there are certain things are are to avoid.

Read: Proverbs 6:1-5

This passage is one of a few that makes a very clear warning against becoming the guarantor for someone else's debt. Solomon says that if one has "*become surety*" for another, it is a matter of great urgency that he free himself of that obligation. He says that one ought to go and beg his neighbor to release him of this obligation even before he gets any more sleep. One who has "*become surety*" for another has been "*snared*" and "*caught*" with the words by which he entered into the agreement. He likens this to a gazelle and a bird that is being hunted. There is no benefit for being the guarantor of another's debt, only suffering (11:15). The guarantor will gain nothing, yet risks his own financial and material loss when others are unwilling or unable to pay their own debts (20:16; 27:13; 22:26-27). So Solomon says, "*He who hates being a guarantor is secure*" (11:15). Being a good steward means we will not unnecessarily risk our own livelihood and security through the lack of good stewardship on the part of others.

Read: Proverbs 22:7

The wise man warns us here against the accumulation of debt. The borrower is under obligation to give a certain amount of the fruits of his labor to the lender. Solomon is not condemning the lender for expecting to be repaid. Rather, he is pointing our the foolishness of entering into a debt obligation unnecessarily. There are times when debt is unavoidable. But the way of the wise is to avoid debt whenever possible and to pay back any debt that exists as quickly as possible, so as to not be under subjection of the entity to which money is owed.

Questions on Lesson 7

1. What lesson does 20:21 teach us about "get rich quick schemes"?

2. Is the negotiating of deals and transactions condemned in 20:14? Explain.

3. What is necessary for one to be able to leave an inheritance to his grand-children (13:22)?

4. By what are we able to survive should the government and economy collapse (27:23-27)?

5. What does 10:22 teach about the source of our blessings?

6. Why does a rich man find himself with more friends than a poor man (14:20; 19:4)?

7. What does 22:7 teach about debt? Does this verse prohibit one from borrowing money under every circumstance? Explain.

Lesson 8

The Application: Alcohol

Key verses: Proverbs 20:1; 23:20-21, 29-35; 31:4-7

Despite the warnings in the book of Proverbs and the rest of the Scriptures against both the destructive and casual uses of alcohol, many claim that a Christian is free to drink alcohol, just so long as he does not become *drunk*. In light of this, it is especially important to note what the book of Proverbs has to say about alcohol.

Read: Proverbs 20:1

Solomon begins this verse by saying, "*Wine is a mocker.*" Alcohol has the ability to make a fool out of someone. It allows one to *think* he is in control when he really is not. The point is made later in the book that alcohol alters the way one thinks (31:5). It is a "*mocker*" to those who believe they can partake in the consumption of alcohol without being affected by it. Next, the wise man says, "*Strong drink* [is] *a brawler.*" This refers to the violent tendencies of one who is given to alcohol and how it causes trouble for both the drinker and those around him. So Solomon says, "*Whoever is intoxicated by it is not wise.*" We have been studying how to *apply* wisdom. If we are to follow the wisdom that comes from above, we must avoid the sin of *drunkenness*.

Read: Proverbs 23:20-21

Solomon groups the sins of drunkenness and gluttony together in these verses. He warns that we should not be "*with*" them, meaning that we should not go along with them so that we put ourselves in a position to be tempted to practice their sins. We cannot avoid all contact with sinful people (cf. 1 Corinthians 5:9-10); but we can avoid putting ourselves in situations in which we will be tempted to give into *peer pressure* and do what others are doing. Furthermore, Solomon makes a point here about *stewardship*. He warns that the "*heavy drinker...will come to poverty.*" Not only is such use of alcohol to be avoided because it has a negative effect upon one's thinking, but also because it is a waste of money.

Solomon's Warning About Alcohol

Read: Proverbs 23:29-35

The above passage contains clear warning from Solomon about the dangers of alcohol. Many will try to justify the casual use of alcohol (often referred to as "*social drinking*"); but given how destructive alcohol can be, Solomon warns that one should not even go this far.

"*Who has woe... sorrow... contentions... complaining... wounds without cause... redness of eyes? Those who linger long over wine, those who go to taste mixed wine*" (23:29-30). Though people often resort to alcohol in an attempt to escape their problems (cf. 31:6-7), Solomon warns that trouble comes to those who "*linger long over wine*" (implying *drunkenness*) and those who "*seek* [KJV] *mixed wine*" (implying the pursuit of alcohol, which would necessarily be *before* drunkenness). The problems caused by alcohol affect every aspect of one's life – emotionally ("*woe*" suggests the idea of *lamentation*); financially ("*sorrow*" is from a word suggesting *want*, in the sense that one comes to be *in need*); socially ("*contentions*" denote the strife and discord that will exist between the drinker and others); verbally ("*complaining*" or "*babbling*" [KJV] refers to the fact that one will not be able to communicate effectively); mentally ("*wounds without cause*" are those wounds one suffers that he cannot recall how he received them because his memory has been affected by the alcohol); and physically ("*redness of eyes*"). Alcohol is not something to be treated lightly.

"*Do not look on the wine when it is red, when it sparkles in the cup, when it goes down smoothly; at the last it bites like a serpent and stings like a viper*" (23:31-32). Those who believe that the casual use of alcohol ("*social drinking*") is acceptable, just so long as one does not proceed to *drunkenness*, need to remember this verse. Rather than advising one to enjoy alcohol in moderation, Solomon warns that one should not even look at it! Though it may *go down smoothly*, it will cause trouble for the one who consumes it. Far from condoning the drinking of alcohol in moderation, Solomon instead warns that one should not even look at it, lest he be tempted to take the first drink.

"*Your eyes will see strange things and your mind will utter perverse things*" (23:33). Alcohol affects one's perception of reality so that he sees "*strange things.*" It also loosens one's tongue so that – rather than filtering out speech that would be improper, offensive, contentious, and unwise – one who consumes alcohol will be more inclined to say those things which should not be said.

"*And you will be like one who lies down in the middle of the sea, or like one who lies down on the top of a mast. 'They struck me, but I did not become ill; they beat me, but I did not know it'*" (23:34-35). Alcohol makes one oblivious to his surroundings (as "*one who lies down in the middle of the sea*") and unaware of any danger in which he may be (as "*one who lies down on the top of a mast*"). Furthermore, alcohol dulls pain ("*they beat me, but I did not know it*") so that the natural reflex to recoil from pain and flee from harm is absent, thus putting the drinker in the position to be harmed even further.

"'*When shall I awake? I will seek another drink*'" (23:35). This phrase reminds us of the addictive nature of alcohol. Despite all the trouble that comes to those who are given to it, many will continue to go back to it.

Warning to Lemuel About Alcohol

Read: Proverbs 31:4-7

This passage is sometimes used by those who want to condone the use of alcohol as a means of dealing with one's problems. Many claim to use alcohol as a way to handle the stress they have from their home, work, or love lives. Yet if we consider the context, there is another point altogether that we should take from this passage.

"It is not for kings, O Lemuel, it is not for kings to drink wine, or for rulers to desire strong drink, for they will drink and forget what is decreed, and pervert the rights of all the afflicted" (31:4-5). First of all, we should note that this instruction is directed toward *kings*. There is a reason behind this. Because a king is in a position of authority over others, there is much more harm that can come from his use of alcohol than others. This passage mentions two reasons why kings and rulers are to avoid alcohol. First, *"they will drink and forget what is decreed"* (31:5). When they forget the difference between right and wrong, it becomes impossible for them to rule effectively or fairly. Second, they will *"pervert the rights of all the afflicted"* (31:5). This does harm to others because it denies them the justice that they deserve. So the admonition is for kings and rulers not to "*drink*" or even "*desire*" alcohol (31:4). The instruction to not "*desire*" it means that the use of alcohol should never even reach the point of casual use ("*social drinking*"), let alone the destructive use (*drunkenness*).

"Give strong drink to him who is perishing, and wine to him whose life is bitter. Let him drink and forget his poverty and remember his trouble no more" (31:6-7). These verses are seen by some as an authorization for the use of alcohol as a way for one to deal with the hardships of life. Yet this does not fit at all with the other passages in Proverbs that identify alcohol as the *cause* of so many hardships in life (23:20-21, 29-35). And while the Bible does authorize the *medicinal* use of alcohol for physical ailments (1 Timothy 5:23), this pas-

sage is talking about mental and emotional hardships. The alcohol, because it alters one's thinking, thus allowing him to *"forget his poverty and remember his trouble no more"* (31:7), is appealing to many. But instead of *authorizing* the practice, this passage simply mentions it as a *common* practice. A practice being *common* certainly does not make it right. The context emphasizes *sober-mindedness* (31:5). One who is to be *sober-minded* – such as the king of this context – must ignore what others are doing, leave them to their devices, and avoid alcohol himself so that he can do what he is responsible to do. Rather than condoning the use of alcohol as a way to forget the troubles of life, this passage teaches us that we must *avoid* alcohol so that we can think clearly and do those things which God would have us to do.

Questions on Lesson 8

1. In what sense is wine a mocker (20:1)?

2. How does the consumption of alcohol relate to the principle of stewardship (23:20-21)?

3. Many argue that the casual use of alcohol is fine as long as one does not become drunk (this idea is often referred to as "social drinking"). Does 23:31 support this idea? Explain.

4. What does alcohol do to one's mental faculties (23:33-35)?

5. What does 23:35 teach about the addictive nature of alcohol?

6. Why are kings and rulers in particular not to drink wine (31:4-5)?

7. Does 31:6-7 authorize the use of alcohol as a way to cope with the hardships of life? Explain. (See also 23:29-30)

Lesson 9

The Application: Women

Key verses: Proverbs 7:1-27; 12:4; 18:22; 5:15-20; 31:10-31

Since much of the book of Proverbs is directed toward the wise man's son, Solomon spends a lot of time discussing women. He warns his son about certain women who are to be avoided. He also gives instruction about the blessings of a good wife and discusses her character so that she might be identified.

Warnings About the Adulteress

Though much of the book of Proverbs contains brief instructions on a broad range of topics, there are several lengthy sections dealing with the dangers of the adulteress (for the sake of space, we will notice just one of these in detail in this chapter; but the related passages should be considered as well). The fact that so much attention to this topic is given in the book of Proverbs should serve as a warning to us about the severe threat that immoral women pose to godly men. So the wise man earnestly pleads with his son to not follow after the adulteress.

Read: Proverbs 7:1-27

"*My son, keep my words and treasure my commandments within you. [...]
That they may keep you from an adulteress, from the foreigner who flatters with
her words*" (7:1-5). Here we have a father issuing a warning to his son about the dangers of the adulteress (cf. 5:1-2; 6:20-24). Certain instructions are often repeated for emphasis. This is certainly a topic that the wise man wants to impress upon his son.

"*For at the window of my house I looked out through my lattice, and I saw among the naive, and discerned among the youths a young man lacking sense"* (7:6-7). The dangers that one may allow himself to experience in his naivete are often observable to others. The wise man talks about being able to see how a young man is getting himself dangerously close to temptation. Yet the young man is oblivious to the trouble that is coming because he is *"lacking sense."* In other words, he has closed his mind to wisdom and is foolishly putting himself in a position to be severely tempted. We need to have enough sense and awareness to avoid temptation whenever possible.

"Passing through the street near her corner; and he takes the way to her house, in the twilight, in the evening, in the middle of the night and in the darkness" (7:8-9). This young man foolishly puts himself in a dangerous situation. He finds himself in the wrong place (*"near her corner;* [on] *the way to her house"*) at the wrong time (*"in the twilight...evening...middle of the night...darkness"*), not by chance, but by choice.

"And behold, a woman comes to meet him, dressed as a harlot and cunning of heart" (7:10). The wise man noted earlier that the adulteress is *actively* trying to capture one in sin – *"An adulteress hunts for the precious life"* (6:26). Here, after the naive young man foolishly takes the way past her house, she seizes the opportunity and goes out to meet him. The first thing he will notice about this woman is her clothing. She wears *"the attire of an harlot"* (KJV), which will only add fuel to the fire of any lustful thoughts he may have. This is deliberate on her part, as she is *"cunning of heart."* But what any woman ought to remember is that if she goes out *"dressed as a harlot,"* wearing clothing that *invites* lust, she has complicity in the sin of one who lusts after her, regardless of whether or not her intention was to seduce him (as was the intention of the harlot).

"She is boisterous and rebellious, her feet do not remain at home; she is now in the streets, now in the squares, and lurks by every corner" (7:11-12). This woman is the opposite of the quiet and submissive wife that was later commended by the apostle Paul (1 Timothy 2:11). The adulteress is *"boisterous and*

rebellious" instead. Solomon says, "*Her feet do not remain at home*" because she is uninterested in the domestic role which God gave to women (Genesis 2:18; Titus 2:4-5).

"So she seizes him and kisses him and with a brazen face she says to him: 'I was due to offer peace offerings; today I have paid my vows. Therefore I have come out to meet you, to seek your presence earnestly, and I have found you. I have spread my couch with coverings, with colored linens of Egypt. I have sprinkled my bed with myrrh, aloes and cinnamon'" (7:13-17). Solomon warns that the adulteress will do everything she can do to make the act of adultery *convenient*. Already she has been described as coming out to the young man, rather than waiting for him to come to her (7:10). She dresses as a harlot in order to incite lust in his heart (7:10). She is wild and rebellious, suggesting that she is interested in fulfilling any worldly and sensual desire she may have, rather than submitting to the will of God (7:11). She is already out in the streets and the squares (7:11-12). Then in these verses, she initiates the affair when she "*seizes him and kisses him*" (7:13). Her statement about peace offerings suggests that, in her mind, she has fulfilled any religious obligation she may have had, thus freeing her time now to do as she pleases (7:14). She makes this young man feel wanted by stating that she has sought him earnestly, while also implying that she is ready for the affair without any persuasions from him (7:15). She has even prepared the place for their sexual encounter ahead of time (7:16-17). She has done whatever she can to remove any roadblock that might delay the affair, reducing the time he might have to realize the terrible mistake he is about to make and flee from her.

"'Come, let us drink our fill of love until morning; let us delight ourselves with caresses'" (7:18). Her offer is appealing to many – to satisfy sexual desires without any long-term commitment. Her invitation is just "*until morning.*" It is all about fulfilling one's *desire* without any sense of *responsibility*.

"'For my husband is not at home, he has gone on a long journey; he has taken a bag of money with him, at the full moon he will come home'" (7:19-20).

One of the dangers of committing adultery with another man's wife is having to later deal with her jealous husband (6:33-35). Yet she convinces the young man that no one will catch them – not even her husband as he has "*gone on a long journey*" and will not be home anytime soon. Of course, even if one's fellow man does not find out, God still knows (cf. Genesis 39:7-10). But in the heat of the moment, one who is being tempted often forgets God. So the promise of not being caught by man becomes very enticing.

"*With her many persuasions she entices him; with her flattering lips she seduces him. Suddenly he follows her as an ox goes to the slaughter, or as one in fetters to the discipline of a fool, until an arrow pierces through his liver; as a bird hastens to the snare, so he does not know that it will cost him his life*" (7:21-23). After all that she does to seduce him, "*Suddenly he follows her*" (7:22). *Suddenly* his will-power gives way to the lust of his heart. Solomon makes no specific mention of the affair after the young man decides to engage in it. It is implied, of course. But it is significant that the time in which they would "*drink* [their] *fill of love until morning*" on her bed "*sprinkled...with myrrh, aloes and cinnamon*" (7:17-18) is completely skipped over in the text. Instead, Solomon goes straight to the consequences of these actions – slaughter, discipline, and a snare. Once sin has been committed and the negative consequences start to take effect, the "*passing pleasures of sin*" (Hebrews 11:25) are suddenly no longer worth mentioning.

"*Now therefore, my sons, listen to me, and pay attention to the words of my mouth. Do not let your heart turn aside to her ways, do not stray into her paths. For many are the victims she has cast down, and numerous are all her slain. Her house is the way of Sheol, descending to the chambers of death*" (7:24-27). The harlot can make adultery convenient, enticing, and seemingly without consequences. But there is no escaping God's judgment. Many have become victims to her. The end result of their sin is death.

Related passages: Proverbs 5:1-14; 6:24-35; 9:13-18; 23:27-28; 29:3; 30:20

* * *

After considering the warnings about the adulteress, we turn our attention to the excellent wife who is commended to us in the book of Proverbs. There are two basic points that are addressed: the blessings and the character of the excellent wife.

The Blessings of a Good Wife

Though the adulteress promises the temporary fulfillment of sexual desires without any long-term commitment (7:18), the wise man makes it clear that it is far better to seek after a good wife than to follow after the adulteress.

Read: Proverbs 12:4

A few of the passages in the book of Proverbs that discuss the blessings of the good wife make a contrast between her and the one who causes trouble for her husband. It is important to note that Solomon is not encouraging his son to marry simply for the sake of getting married. A wife who "*shames*" her husband "*is like rottenness to his bones.*" There are some women who – because of their godless, contentious, and self-absorbed character – are not worthy of consideration when one is looking for a spouse. But an "*excellent wife*" – if one is patient enough to find her – "*is the crown of her husband.*"

Read: Proverbs 18:22

Remembering what Solomon says in the verse previously considered (12:4), the wife being discussed in this verse is not just any wife but is the *excellent* wife. In the next chapter, the wise man says, "*House and wealth are an inheritance from fathers, but a prudent wife is from the Lord*" (19:14). One who finds such a blessing "*obtains favor from the Lord.*" God instituted marriage in the beginning (Genesis 2:18-24). Therefore, all blessings that come from the marriage relationship are possible because of God's perfect plan for man and woman.

Read: Proverbs 21:9; 27:15-16

Peter spoke of the "*holy women*" who lived long ago who were "*submissive to their own husbands; just as Sarah obeyed Abraham, calling him lord*" (1 Peter 3:5-6). God has placed the responsibility of submission upon women from the beginning when he created Eve to be "*a helper suitable for*" Adam (Genesis 2:18). The "*contentious woman*" is the opposite of the submissive wife. She is like the "*constant dripping on a day of steady rain*" by being a source of regular aggravation for him. Through the nagging, bickering, ridicule, antagonism, and strife she forces her husband to endure, she makes it so that he might think that he would be better off living "*in a corner of a roof*" (21:9; 25:24) or "*in a desert land*" (21:19), rather than with her. A contentious woman makes it so that it is impossible to have harmony in the home because she arrogantly wants her way rather than submitting to her husband as his "*help meet*" (Genesis 2:18, KJV).

Read: Proverbs 5:15-20

God designed marriage as the relationship in which a man and a woman can fulfill their sexual desires (Genesis 2:24; Hebrews 13:4). Solomon's advice to his son in these verses is that he should be *content* with his wife in regard to their sexual relationship (5:15). He was not to seek out the adulteress (5:20); he warned his son about her in other passages (5:1-14; 6:24-35; 7:1-27; 9:13-18). He warns his son not to let his "*springs be dispersed abroad*" (5:16), dividing his attention, support, care, and affections between his wife (to whom they should exclusively be directed) and others. He says, "*Let your fountain be blessed*" (5:18). A *fountain* refers to a *source*. In this context, it is the source of his life, which is his heart (cf. 4:23). His heart and his life will be blessed as he rejoices "*in the wife of* [his] *youth*" (5:18). He is to enjoy their sexual relationship and "*be exhilarated always with her love*" (5:19). Pursuing sexual desires outside of marriage only leads to trouble. Fulfilling sexual desires within marriage, as God intended, is a great blessing.

Related passages: Proverbs 11:16, 22; 14:1

The Character of the Excellent Wife

Many read the passage in Proverbs 31 of the "*excellent wife*" or the "*virtuous woman*" (KJV) and assume that the wise man is describing the ideal woman who does not exist in reality. However, even though culture and technology have changed since the time of the book of Proverbs, the "*excellent wife*" today is going to have the same focus as the one described in the following passage – fearing God, supporting her husband, serving her family, and helping others. There can be no change in culture or technology that would rightly call for a shift in focus from these four fundamental areas. Rather than think of the "*excellent wife*" of Proverbs 31 as an ideal that only exists in abstract terms, women today must look at her and see how they might imitate her in their lives.

Read: Proverbs 31:10-31

"*An excellent wife, who can find? For her worth is far above jewels*" (31:10). In asking the question – "*Who can find?*" – the wise man is not saying that "*an excellent wife*" cannot be found. Rather, he is emphasizing the fact that such a wife is rare and is therefore "*worth...far above jewels.*" Therefore, because she is so valuable, she ought to be treated as such.

"*The heart of her husband trusts in her, and he will have no lack of gain. She does him good and not evil all the days of her life*" (31:11-12). As a suitable "*help meet*" (Genesis 2:18, KJV), the *excellent wife* seeks to support her husband, rather than selfishly pursue her own ambitions and desires. Because of her consistency in this, her husband is able to *trust in her*; and he will prosper. One of her primary focuses is that she "*does him good and not evil all the days of her life.*"

"*She looks for wool and flax and works with her hands in delight*" (31:13). Adam Clarke, in his commentary, points out that the wool and flax this woman seeks for her work is not ready woven cloth but the raw material that has likely come from her own flocks and fields. This suggests that the *excellent wife* is willing to work harder, rather than take short cuts, when it is prudent to do so. She is not only able but *willing* to work with her hands. She does so not grudgingly but with joy.

"*She is like merchant ships; she brings her food from afar*" (31:14). The merchant ships would be engaged in buying, selling, and trading. The *excellent wife* is like them in that she is able to obtain food for her household through the goods she produces that she is able to bring to the market (cf. 31:24). She is also willing to bring "*food from afar*," signifying the fact that her thoughts revolve around what is best for her family, not what is most convenient for her.

"*She rises also while it is still night and gives food to her household and portions to her maidens*" (31:15). The fact that the *excellent wife* has maidens (servants) who work for her should not lead us to discount all the work that she does as being non-applicable to women today. In fact, we see that the *excellent wife* makes the most of her time in that she "*rises...while it is still night*" and sees to it that these maidens have the provisions (*food*) and assignments (*portions*) they will need for the day ahead.

"*She considers a field and buys it; from her earnings she plants a vineyard*" (31:16). Earlier the wise man says that this woman's husband "*trusts in her, and he will have no lack of gain*" (31:11). The *excellent wife* is willing to spend money. Yet she does not spend money selfishly on her own desires. Instead, she carefully considers a field and buys it as an investment to contribute to the family. "*She plants a vineyard*" from the money she earns through the sale of those products she makes with her own hands (31:24).

"*She girds herself with strength and makes her arms strong*" (31:17). E. M. Zerr's comments on this verse are helpful: "This woman puts a belt around her waist, not for show or ornament, but to assist her in her work for the family." She "*makes her arms strong*" so that she will be ready and able to carry out the various tasks that are necessary in taking care of her household.

"*She senses that her gain is good; her lamp does not go out at night*" (31:18). The *excellent wife* sees profit in the work that she does. With this positive outlook, she carries out her responsibilities, even though it often means working long hours – into the night – to care for her house.

"*She stretches out her hands to the distaff, and her hands grasp the spindle*" (31:19). This is connected with the verse earlier that describes the *excellent wife* as looking "*for wool and flax and* [working] *with her hands in delight*" (31:13).

"*She extends her hand to the poor, and she stretches out her hands to be needy*" (31:20). This woman is not only concerned with her family. She is also eager to help those who are less fortunate. Because of the work that she does, she is in a position to provide aid for them.

"*She is not afraid of the snow for her household, for all her household are clothed with scarlet. She makes coverings for herself; her clothing is fine linen and purple*" (31:21-22). The *excellent wife* makes preparations so that her household is well-equipped to handle even challenging circumstances. "*She is not afraid of the snow*" because she prepares for it. The wise man specifically mentions her making clothing for herself. She also supplies clothing for her household, either by making it herself or by obtaining it through the fruit of her labor.

"*Her husband is known in the gates, when he sits among the elders of the land*" (31:23). Being "*known in the gates*" and sitting "*among the elders of the land*" is an indication that her husband is in a place of honor and respect. This is made possible, in part, by having a good *"help meet"* (Genesis 2:18, KJV) who very capably fulfills her responsibilities within the home so that he can focus on his responsibilities outside of the home.

"She makes linen garments and sells them, and supplies belts to the tradesmen" (31:24). This woman is more than willing to contribute to her household's income. She does so, not by leaving the home to find work elsewhere, but by doing work that is an extension of the work she is already doing within her role in the home (cf. 31:13, 19, 21-22).

"Strength and dignity are her clothing, and she smiles at the future" (31:25). The clothing mentioned here is figurative and describes her character. Because of her character, industriousness, and wise stewardship, she is able to look optimistically toward the future. As the wise man later mentions the fact that she *"fears the Lord"* (31:30), we can also conclude that this optimism she has is rooted in her faith in God.

"She opens her mouth in wisdom, and the teaching of kindness is on her tongue" (31:26). The *excellent wife* is not only busy working with her hands and taking care of the needs of her household, she is also active in teaching others. The wisdom she teaches is not worldly wisdom, but the wisdom that comes from above. She also teaches kindness, which ought to be expected, given how she treats others.

"She looks well to the ways of her household, and does not eat the bread of idleness" (31:27). Most of this passage about the *excellent wife* describes how the she focuses on her household. This is one of her primary concerns. There are many responsibilities that come with this; so as she *"looks well to the ways of her household,"* she is diligent in her labor. The stereotype of the lazy housewife is nothing like the woman of this passage.

"Her children rise up and bless her; her husband also, and he praises her, saying: 'Many daughters have done nobly, but you excel them all'" (31:28-29). As

her focus is largely directed toward her household, particularly her husband and children, these are the ones who rise up to bless and praise her. Her husband recognizes that when compared with other women, she *excels them all.* She is a rare treasure (31:10); and he recognizes this, as every husband of an *excellent wife* should as well.

"*Charm is deceitful and beauty is vain, but a woman who fears the Lord, she shall be praised*" (31:30). The world values charm and beauty. Yet for one to appreciate this *excellent wife*, he must understand what is truly important. Charm only deceives one into believing that someone is better than her character would indicate. Physical beauty means little. But this woman is worthy of praise because she "*fears the Lord.*" Though her service to God is barely mentioned in this passage, all the work that she does in supporting her husband, serving her family, and helping others indicates that she has a strong desire to serve the Lord and fulfill the responsibilities He has given her in the role of a wife and mother.

"*Give her the product of her hands, and let her works praise her in the gates*" (31:31). The *excellent wife* is worthy of honor, respect, and gratitude for all the work that she does. This praise is not private, and certainly not unspoken. Instead, the praise she is due ought to be public ("*in the gates*") so that all can recognize her devotion and follow her godly example.

Questions on Lesson 9

1. Why does Solomon contrast the hungry thief with the one who commits adultery with another man's wife (6:30-35)?

2. What does it mean for a woman dress as a harlot (7:10)?

3. What does Solomon describe the adulteress as doing to make adultery convenient (7:10-20)?

4. Why does the husband of the *"excellent wife"* trust in her (31:10-12)?

5. What does the excellent wife do for her household (31:13-27)?

6. Why is it significant that her husband was "*among the elders of the land*" (31:23)?

7. In 31:30, the excellent wife is counted as worthy of praise because she "*fears the Lord.*" What does this suggest about the connection between a woman fearing God and her work for her household?

Lesson 10

The Application: Family

Key verses: Proverbs 15:17; 17:1; 20:7; 22:6, 15; 17:2, 6; 13:22

The first and primary human relationship was that of the man and woman in marriage (Genesis 2:18-24). From this relationship came the first children (Genesis 4:1-2); and all mankind descended from there (Acts 17:26). The book of Proverbs contains several instructions about family relationships, emphasizing the importance of harmony in the home, as well as responsibilities of parents, children, and grandparents.

Harmony in the Home

Read: Proverbs 15:17; 17:1

A poor family is able to sustain itself on little more than a "*dish of vegetables*" and a "*dry morsel.*" While such a condition may not be desirable in itself, Solomon makes the point that if there is *love* and *quietness* (the absence of strife) within a home, poverty can be endured. More than that, the prosperity that allows one to enjoy *feasting* is not worth pursuing if it leads to *hatred* and *strife* within the home. Too many people sacrifice family in order to pursue success in the things of this life. But no amount of this world's wealth can replace the blessing of harmony in the home.

Read: Proverbs 10:1; 17:25

A foolish son, by rejecting the ways of wisdom and being concerned only with fulfilling his desires, will cause trouble in the home. He causes grief to both father (17:25) and mother (10:1). By his selfish and rebellious actions, he demonstrates that he "*despises his mother*" (15:20). Rather than helping to preserve harmony in the family, the foolish son instead brings about "*destruction*" (19:13).

Read: Proverbs 17:21

The joy that accompanies the birth of a child does not always last. As the child grows, if he does not follow the path of wisdom, heeding the instruction of his parents, the "*foolishness*" that is "*bound up in* [his] *heart*" (22:15) will take root and will define his life. One is not a fool from conception or birth but becomes one as he chooses the paths of wickedness. The father of such a one loses the joy he once experienced on account of his child, and it is replaced with sorrow.

Related passages: Proverbs 23:15-16, 24-25; 27:11

To the Parents

Read: Proverbs 20:7

When one follows God as he ought to, not only will he be blessed (cf. 11:3-8), but his children will be blessed as well. First of all, as God *delights* in those who follow Him, a secondary benefit is that "*the descendants of the righteous will be delivered*" (11:20-21). Second, the children of the righteous man are blessed in that they have his good example to follow. Third, the children of the righteous man are blessed because they are taught by him "*in the way* [they] *should go*" (22:6).

Read: Proverbs 22:6

The statement in this verse is one that is *generally* true. Certainly, because man has free will, it is possible for parents to teach their children as they ought to and then, when their children have grown, they forsake the paths of righteousness. But generally speaking, when parents lead their children in the way of truth, they will continue in it in their adult life. So the influence of the parents is not limited to the home prior to the children reaching adulthood. Therefore, parents must seriously consider their responsibility in teaching their children.

Read: Proverbs 22:15

Foolishness is used two different ways in the book of Proverbs. It can refer to the state of merely *lacking* knowledge. It can also refer to the state of *willful rejection* of knowledge. The former is the type of foolishness in the heart of a child. A child simply *lacks* knowledge and needs to be trained. Part of this training involves discipline. This is not referring to verbal reprimands – though there are times when verbal instruction is necessary – but *corporal punishment.* Solomon makes this clear because he does not just mention *discipline* but the "*rod of discipline.*"

Read: Proverbs 13:24

Those who refuse to use *corporal punishment* in the discipline of children believe they are acting in love. Yet Solomon says that the one who "*withholds his rod*" – by failing to administer this type of discipline – "*hates his son.*" Therefore, the one who loves his son will discipline him *diligently.* The word translated *diligently* means to seek *early* or *earnestly.* The point is that while parents must discipline their children in earnest, they must also do so in a timely manner. This means that from an early age, parents ought to discipline their children appropriately so that the children learn early in life that there are consequences for failing to obey.

Read: Proverbs 19:18

Solomon says that discipline must be administered "*while there is hope.*"

The implication is that the time may come when there is no hope. The age in which a child's heart becomes hardened and unreceptive to the instruction of his parents will vary. Parents should then discipline their children *diligently* – earnestly and early [see comments on 13:24] – so that this point is never reached. The New American Standard version says: "*Do not desire his death.*" This suggests that discipline must always be done in love as an effort to train a child, not as a reaction in anger. The King James Version is worded a little differently: "*Let not thy soul spare for his crying.*" The type of discipline that Solomon refers to here (*corporal punishment*) will often result in the child *crying*. Parents should not allow this to deter them in their efforts to administer proper discipline. Solomon explains this in the following verse.

Related passages: Proverbs 23:13-14; 29:15, 17

To the Children

Read: Proverbs 17:2

This verse could be used to emphasize the hard work and dedication of the servant. However, there is another point to be made about the son that Solomon mentions. The fact that he is a son does not mean that his shameful actions will be overlooked. Being a son does not mean that one should feel entitled to anything that his parents have. Solomon specifically mentions the inheritance in this verse. While it is often true that a child will receive an inheritance from his parents, he should not act as though he has an exclusive right to what does not yet belong to him. Too many young people in our society develop an unhealthy sense of *entitlement*. Yet parents can use their resources as they see fit – even by leaving an inheritance to a wise servant. Rather than having a sense of entitlement, children of all ages should learn *humility*, walk *righteously*, and *honor* their parents.

Read: Proverbs 28:24

This verse also deals with the entitlement mentality that many children have. They believe that they *deserve* whatever might belong to their parents, even before their parents might decide to freely give anything to them. So these wicked children feel as though they can *rob* their parents without doing anything wrong. The wise man notes how serious this crime is when he says that the one who would do this is "*the companion of a man who destroys.*"

Read: Proverbs 30:11, 17

The most fundamental command for children is the fifth of the Ten Commandments: "*Honor your father and your mother, that your days may be prolonged in the land which the Lord your God gives you*" (Exodus 20:12). With this command came the promise that God would bless them in the land they were receiving. The verses above explain that those who fail to honor their parents will not only miss out on the blessings that come from obedience to this command but will suffer a disgraceful punishment for their sins.

Related passage: Proverbs 19:26

To the Grandparents

Read: Proverbs 17:6

A crown is a sign that one is deserving of honor and respect. Having grandchildren is also a sign that one is worthy of such honor and respect. In order to have grandchildren, a grandparent must first raise his own children in such a way that they are capable of raising their children (his grandchildren).

Read: Proverbs 13:22

This verse is not talking about a guaranteed outcome. One may be a good man, but on account of circumstances beyond his control, has nothing to leave as an inheritance to his children, let alone his grandchildren. Instead, this verse is talking about the fact that a good man will have the necessary characteristics that might allow him to leave an inheritance to his grandchildren – hard work, good stewardship, and a concern for future generations. Circumstances in life may not always work out as one would hope, but all men ought to have these qualities.

Questions on Lesson 10

1. Is harmony in the home to be sacrificed for prosperity (15:17; 17:1)?

2. What does 27:11 suggest about the connection between a child's actions and his parent's reputation?

3. Is 22:6 an absolute statement? Explain.

4. What is bound up in a child's heart and how is it removed (22:15)?

5. What does 29:15 say about a child who gets his own way?

6. Is a child permitted to rob his parents (28:24) Explain.

7. In what way are grandchildren the crown of old men (17:6)?

Lesson 11

The Application: Friendship

Key verses: Proverbs 17:17; 27:17; 24:1-2; 18:24; 13:20; 1:10-19

Beyond the family, the next closest relationship that one has is with his friends. The companions with whom one chooses to associate have a great influence upon his thinking and behavior. Therefore, it is important for one to choose his friends wisely. The book of Proverbs contains instructions that will help us see the reason why good friends are so important and why bad friends are so dangerous.

The Value of Good Friends

Read: Proverbs 17:17

Because of the family ties that exist, a brother can often be counted upon in times of adversity. On the other hand, a friend – the companion one has by *choice*, rather than by *birth* – can be counted upon for support and encouragement "*at all times,*" not just during times of hardship. It should be noted that the *friend* of this verse is a *true friend*. Sadly, many "friends" are not. These will be discussed later on.

Read: Proverbs 27:6

Because we are imperfect, we often need correction. The wounds of a friend are "*faithful*" because they are designed to correct and guide one back to the truth. Unlike the friend, one's enemy does not have his best interest at heart. Therefore, the "*kisses*" that the enemy offers – signs of affection, approval, and encouragement – are "*deceitful*" because they give one the impression that he is fine in his current state. Though the *"wounds of a friend"* may be temporarily painful, they are ultimately helpful as they allow one to see his sin and make correction. A true friend is willing to do this, rather than attempting to make one feel comfortable in sin as the enemy does.

Read: Proverbs 27:17

One of the things that good friends do for one another is that they help make each other better. A good friend is not going to encourage one to remain in sin or to be content with mediocrity. Instead, a good friend is going to encourage one to become more like God and continue to follow the path of wisdom.

Related passage: Proverbs 27:9

The Danger of Bad Friends

Compared to the passages that discuss the value of good friends, there are many more that warn about the danger of bad friends. A possible reason for this is that man generally understands that friendship is important but is not always as discerning in choosing his friends as he ought to be. Therefore, a greater emphasis is placed upon the warnings. So let us consider the warnings in the book of Proverbs about bad friendships.

Read: Proverbs 24:1-2

We are not to envy evil men because their ultimate fate is one of destruction when the time comes for God to *"render to man according to his work"* (24:12). In addition to this warning, Solomon says that we should not *"desire to be with them"* because of their corrupt thoughts, speech, and, by implication, actions. Friends are those close companions we *choose* for ourselves. It is imperative that we be very careful not to choose those who are evil.

Read: Proverbs 14:7

Those with whom we associate will have an influence upon us. The longer we associate with fools, the more likely we will start seeing things from their perspective. As fools *despise...wisdom* (23:9), we will, on account of their influence, cease discerning the words of knowledge as well.

Read: Proverbs 24:21-22

In choosing one's companions, it is important to do so in the fear of God. Solomon couples this with the fear one ought to have for the king. Because of this connection, we must understand this ruler to be one who is ruling according to the will of God. This is why he says, "*Do not associate with those who are given to change.*" Change can be good, particularly if sin and corruption need to be corrected. If rulers are acting contrary to the will of God, we ought to desire change in this regard. But change for the sake of change – which is what Solomon is referring to here – is not good. It reflects an attitude of rebellion and discontent. Seeking change for these reasons, rather than for principles of righteousness, will lead one not only to resist civil leaders, but God as well. Those who have such a rebellious and discontented heart will face calamity "*suddenly.*" Therefore, one who is following the path of wisdom will avoid "*those who are given to change.*"

Read: Proverbs 18:24

The New American Standard and King James translations are very different for the first half of this verse. One says, "*A man of too many friends comes to ruin*" (NASB). The other says, "*A man that hath friends must shew himself friendly*" (KJV). The point suggested in the King James Version is the one most think of when reading this verse – if one expects to have friends, he must show himself to be friendly to others. This is true. But the wording in the New American Standard suggests that this refers to more than just showing good will toward others. Instead, one who has "*too many friends*" must try to please them all – a nearly impossible task. Therefore, Solomon says this man "*comes to ruin.*" On the other hand, there is "*a friend*" (as opposed to "*many friends*") who "*sticks closer than a brother.*" This is a true friend. Friends like this are sometimes difficult to find. But rather than trying to please everyone – which will only result in making everyone unhappy in one way or another – the wise man will recognize who his true friends are, though they may be few, and not allow himself to ruined by all the others.

Read: Proverbs 19:4, 6-7

The friends discussed in these verses are not like the "*friend who sticks closer than a brother*" (18:24). These are not true friends but are only interested in taking advantage of others. This is why they flock to those who are wealthy and generous, but they forsake those who are poor. True friends will show a genuine interest in the *person*, regardless of his economic status.

Read: Proverbs 27:14

This verse teaches us of the need to be considerate of others. The fact that a *blessing* is given is irrelevant if it comes at such a time and in a certain way as to cause stress and annoyance to the one being blessed. We should be thoughtful of others and not assume that every supposed kindness that we might show in every circumstance and in every way will be welcome.

Related passages: Proverbs 17:12; 22:24-25; 28:7; 29:24; 23:6-8; 20:19; 22:10

The Power of Peer Pressure

Peer pressure is not a phenomenon that affects only those who are still in their youth. All people, young and old, can be influenced by their peers. This influence could be either good or bad.

Read Proverbs 13:20

Those who choose to keep company with "*wise men*" will learn from them and become wise themselves. On the other hand, those who choose to keep company with "*fools*" will suffer the fate of fools. Therefore, companions must be chosen carefully. In the following passage, Solomon warns of the dangerous influence and peer pressure that comes from evil companions.

Read: Proverbs 1:10-19

"*My son, if sinners entice you, do not consent*" (1:10). Though Solomon says "*if*," he does not mean that sinners might leave some people alone and not try to influence them. Sinners *will* try to draw others into their ungodly activities. When this happens, the wise man states simply and clearly, "*Do not consent.*"

"*If they say, 'Come with us, let us lie in wait for blood, let us ambush the innocent without cause; let us swallow them alive like Sheol, even whole, as those who go down to the pit'*" (1:11-12). Those who find enjoyment in doing harm to others are not the kind of friends we ought to have. While those who would try to "*entice*" us will often not propose such extreme and aggressive actions, a similar attitude of contempt for one's fellow man is common today. We should avoid those who have such an attitude.

"*'We will find all kinds of precious wealth, we will fill our houses with spoil; throw in your lot with us, we shall all have one purse'*" (1:13-14). In their wicked activities, those who would tempt us will offer a share in the spoils of their sin. This carries with it the idea of *fellowship*. Yet if one wishes to share in the *spoil* of sin, he must also share in the *punishment* of sin (1:19).

"*My son, do not walk in the way with them. Keep your feet from their path, for their feet run to evil and they hasten to shed blood*" (1:15-16). The ones about whom Solomon warns his son are not simply misguided youths who end up in the wrong place at the wrong time. Evil does not just happen to find them; they go out looking for it. Therefore, if one walks "*in the way with them*," he will find himself in the same trouble.

"*Indeed, it is useless to spread the baited net in the sight of any bird; but they lie in wait for their own blood; they ambush their own lives. So are the ways of everyone who gains by violence; it takes away the life of its possessors*" (1:17-19). Though their intention is to take advantage of and harm others, these wicked ones are ultimately destroying themselves. Sin always tempts one to focus on the short-term gain and ignore the long-term consequences. Often, one can see the long-term consequences if he will simply pay attention. Solomon says, "*It is useless to spread the baited net in the sight of any bird.*" Why? The bird will see it and not fall for the trap. But often, sinners foolishly see, but ignore, the damaging effects of their sin. They will suffer for it. If we consent to go with them (1:10), we will suffer as well.

Related passage: Proverbs 4:14-19

Questions on Lesson 11

1. Explain the difference between a friend and a brother (17:17).

2. How does one man sharpen another (27:17)?

3. Why must one leave the presence of a fool (14:7)?

4. Why should one not associate with a gossip (20:19)?

5. Why does "*a man of too many friends* [come] *to ruin*" (18:24)?

6. What will happen to one who "*walks with wise men*" (13:20)?

7. Does peer pressure affect only young people? Explain.

Lesson 12

The Application: Neighbors

Key verses: Proverbs 3:27-28; 24:29; 20:3; 10:12; 17:13-14; 14:21, 31

We have already studied what the book of Proverbs teaches about our relationships with family and friends. But there are many people we interact with on a regular basis that are outside of these relationships. So let us consider the words of wisdom about our dealings with *neighbors.*

Do Good to Others

Read: Proverbs 3:27-28

There may be circumstances in which we are simply unable to do good to others. Paul told the Corinthians that God judges one's performance of good works toward others "*according to what a person has, not according to what he does not have*" (2 Corinthians 8:12). But while there are legitimate reasons why a person may not be able to help his neighbor, there are other reasons that are merely excuses. One will always be able to find an excuse for refusing to do good. When we have the ability and opportunity to help others, we ought to just do it.

Read: Proverbs 24:17-18

We are not to find joy in the suffering of others. Even when one is suffering on account of his own sin, we are not to rejoice over this. The consequences and punishment for sin are what Solomon refers to in this passage, as he says that our rejoicing may cause God's "*anger* [to] *turn away from him.*" More than this, our rejoicing will cause God's anger that was directed at our neighbor to be turned against us. This is implied in this passage but stated explicitly elsewhere: "*He who rejoices at calamity will not go unpunished*" (17:5).

Read: Proverbs 24:29

This passage is the opposite of the well-known "Golden Rule" given by Jesus: "*In everything, therefore, treat people the same way you want them to treat you, for this is the Law and the Prophets*" (Matthew 7:12). Man often has a tendency to retaliate for what someone else has done to him. Yet the one who walks in wisdom will reject this carnal inclination and do good to others, regardless of how he is treated by them.

Read: Proverbs 25:21-22

Paul quoted this passage in Romans 12:19-20 to encourage Christians to leave vengeance to God. In that passage, the apostle also quoted from the Law of Moses: "*Vengeance is Mine, and retribution, in due time their foot will slip*" (Deuteronomy 32:35). We should seek to do good to others, rather than take vengeance into our own hands. We can trust in God that He will handle any punishment that is necessary for the transgressor.

Read: Proverbs 27:10

The wise man counsels one to not go to his brother "*in the day of calamity.*" The reason for this is that his brother is "*far away.*" When the need for help is urgent, there is no time to wait for aid that might come from a distant relative. It is better to have "*a neighbor who is near*" who would be able to come to the aid of one in distress. This verse implies that one ought to be willing to provide help to his neighbor when such help is necessary.

Related passages: Proverbs 3:29; 12:26; 29:5; 24:11; 11:10-11; 29:21

Seek Peace

Read: Proverbs 20:3

Just as the wicked man *"desires evil"* and is looking for some reason to be critical of his neighbor (21:10), the fool is looking for some reason to argue with his neighbor. Though there are certainly occasions that warrant honorable discussion and debate, the fool seeks to argue for the sake of arguing. The honorable course is to avoid strife whenever possible.

Read: Proverbs 25:8-10

Too often, men foolishly desire to make their private quarrel with a neighbor known to others. Yet when we have a complaint against someone in a personal or private matter, we ought to go to that person first and try to resolve the issue. Instead, if we immediately turn our private dispute into a public quarrel, we may be humiliated and receive reproach if we are found to be in the wrong. Better to keep private matters private whenever possible, rather than risk our own reputation and threaten any hope of future peace with our neighbor.

Read: Proverbs 18:19

It is often very difficult to repair a damaged relationship. Solomon uses the analogy of capturing a strong city to illustrate this point. Though this is a difficult task, it is easier than trying to win back one who has been offended. The *"contentions"* that arise between brethren *"are like the bars of a citadel,"* keeping out those who are unwelcome – such as the offending brother. We should take care not to damage our relationships with others. Often these severed ties are difficult to restore. Sometimes the damage is irreparable.

Read: Proverbs 25:17

In trying to be good neighbors, some will take it upon themselves to visit and spend time with them to show their neighbors that they value their relationship. Often this is done with the best of intentions, but Solomon offers a word of caution in this verse. What is often done with good intentions can be interpreted much differently by one's neighbor. While it is good to be friendly, we also need to respect the privacy of others and not impose when we are unwelcome. If a neighbor invites us into his home, we must be careful not to overstay our welcome, lest the good feelings he has for us become exhausted and he learns to resent us.

Read: Proverbs 26:17

"*One who takes a dog by the ears*" provokes the animal to anger and causes it to turn against him when it may have otherwise ignored him. This is the same thing that one does when he takes it upon himself to meddle in the business of others. When the meddling (often thought to be "helpful" by the meddler) is unwelcome, it will cause the ones involved in the strife to turn against him.

Read: Proverbs 26:18-19

The word *madman* is from a root word which suggests the idea of being *rabid* or *insane*. Solomon describes one who is not in control of his mind; therefore, the arrows he shoots, rather than hitting a target, will go in random directions, causing damage to people or things that were never intended as targets. One who deceives his neighbor, but afterward claims to have been "*joking*," will cause far more damage than he intended, damage which cannot be undone.

Related passages: Proverbs 17:19; 21:10; 16:29

* * *

There will be times in which a neighbor commits wrong against us. The following passages provide instruction for such cases.

Read: Proverbs 10:12; 15:18

When a neighbor sins against us, it is important that we respond appropriately. The appropriate response is not to retaliate, as this will only cause the situation to escalate. If we respond with a *hot-temper* and *hatred*, we will only make the strife worse. Instead, we ought to respond with love and patience, hoping to find a peaceful resolution. If a neighbor sins against us, escalating the tensions and strife will only drive our neighbor further into sin. By showing love and patience, we may be able to later influence him toward the ways of God.

* * *

There will also be times in which a neighbor does no wrong to us. However, too often we are tempted to treat him poorly anyway. The following passages warn against doing this.

Read: Proverbs 3:30; 24:28; 30:10; 17:13-14

We must not contend with (3:30), be a witness against (24:28), or speak evil against (30:10) anyone *without cause*. Yes, there are times when it is necessary to contend with, testify against, and offer a report against someone. But if someone has done nothing wrong, it is foolish of us to oppose him. By returning *"evil for good"* in this way, we only invite trouble for ourselves, as *"evil will not depart from"* our houses (17:13). Solomon goes on and says, *"The beginning of strife is like letting out water"* (17:14). Once the floodgates are opened by our unjust accusations, it is difficult to correct the situation. If others have done no wrong, we must not turn against them.

Help the Poor

Read: Proverbs 14:21

After noting the passages that speak of our responsibility to do good to others and seek for peace with our neighbors, the first phrase of this verse fits with those ideas. In the second part of this verse, Solomon specifically talks about one's dealings with *"the poor."* One who is gracious will be *happy* (blessed by God).

Read: Proverbs 19:17; 22:9

One who provides help to the poor will rarely receive recompense from those whom he helps. But one who gives to the poor ought not do so with the hope of receiving repayment from him. Instead, in helping the poor he *"lends to the Lord."* God, who is the giver of all good things (cf. James 1:17), will *"repay him for his good deed."* As with many of the proverbs, this is not to be interpreted to mean that if we use some of our money to help the poor then God will return even more money back to us. The blessings that God provides are not limited to financial and material things. God is able to bless us even after this life. Paul later told Timothy to instruct the rich to *"do good, to be rich in good works, to be generous and ready to share, storing up for themselves the treasure of a good foundation for the future, so that they may take hold of that which is life indeed"* (1 Timothy 6:18-19). The *"life indeed"* they were to focus on as their reward for doing good to others was eternal life.

Read: Proverbs 21:13

This is much like Jesus' point about forgiveness: *"For if you forgive others for their transgressions, your heavenly Father will also forgive you. But if you do not forgive others, then your Father will not forgive your transgressions"* (Matthew 6:14-15). The same principle is used by Solomon in this passage. One who is *"gracious to a poor man"* will be blessed by God (19:17; 22:9). But one who refuses to help when he has the ability and opportunity to do so will be abandoned by God.

Read: Proverbs 14:31; 17:5

Both the acts of *oppressing* and *mocking* the poor are like taunting God. Helping the poor honors God (14:31). Rejoicing in the plight of the poor will result in divine punishment. A few chapters later, Solomon makes a related point: *"Do not rob the poor because he is poor, or crush the afflicted at the gate; for the Lord will plead their case and take the life of those who rob them"* (22:22-23). God is a fair, righteous, and omniscient judge. One who abuses the poor will not escape punishment.

Related passages: Proverbs 22:16; 28:3

Questions on Lesson 12

1. How does one spread a net for someone through flattery (29:5)?

2. Why does a city rejoice *"when it goes well with the righteous"* (11:10-11)?

3. Why should one not hastily argue his case against his neighbor (25:8-10)?

4. Why does Solomon say, *"Let your foot rarely be in your neighbor's house"* (25:17)?

5. What is the consequence for one who *"returns evil for good"* (17:13-14)?

6. In what sense does one who is *"gracious to a poor man"* lend to the Lord (19:17)?

7. How does our attitude toward the poor affect God's attitude toward us (21:13)?

Lesson 13

The Application: Government

Key verses: Proverbs 14:34; 28:2; 20:8, 26; 14:28; 17:26; 28:4; 24:21; 29:26

Given the way people talk about government as it relates to the Scriptures, many might assume that there is very little in the way of instruction regarding government in the book of Proverbs. Yet there are quite a few passages that teach us about government, as well as providing instructions both to those in government and those who are subject to governing authorities. We begin with the following verse: "*Righteousness exalts a nation, but sin is a disgrace to any people*" (14:34).

Though this passage is not *specifically* referring to civil government, there are certainly principles that will apply. A nation will be exalted before God due to the righteousness of the people. Therefore, those in authority ought to encourage righteousness. This will be done primarily by directing the force and wrath of government's power toward the wicked and away from the righteous. Solomon also says that sin among the people brings shame upon the nation. Therefore, those in authority should not support or encourage wickedness among the people.

About Government: Its Place and Role

Read: Proverbs 28:2

E.M. Zerr explained the significance of the *many princes* in his comments on this verse: "A prince is a leading person without official authority as a general thing. Such men are brought into prominence by the misdoings of a country. But one man of substantial kind of knowledge will ensure the state of a nation." These *princes* that arise through the transgressions of the people will threaten the long-term health of the nation. They consume the country's resources while doing nothing to fulfill the government's God-given role. Actual *"understanding and knowledge"* are far more important contributions that one might make for the health of a nation than merely holding some official position.

Read: Proverbs 16:14-15

The king, in his role as the head of civil authority, holds the power of life and death over the people he rules (cf. 19:12). Unfortunately, this verse says nothing about the justice incumbent on the king in punishing or rewarding his subjects. For this reason, several passages in Proverbs emphasize the need for kings to rule with *justice*. Yet the characteristic that exists in all human government is not *justice*, but *power*.

Read: Proverbs 20:8

Being in a position of power, God expects rulers to establish their thrones on *justice*. If a ruler does this, evil will be dispersed because justice demands that wickedness be punished.

Read: Proverbs 20:26

One of the primary responsibilities that government has is to punish those who do evil. The King James Version says, *"A wise king scattereth the wicked,"* again emphasizing the fact that a ruler acting according to his divinely-given role will be a cause of fear for those who do evil. On the other hand, this also implies that when a government refuses to punish wickedness as it ought, sin will abound.

Read: Proverbs 28:28; 29:2

The wise man implies that the ones who "*hide themselves*" from wicked rulers are not other wicked persons who deserve punishment. Righteous kings punish the wicked (20:8, 26); wicked kings do not. Instead, wicked kings are a cause of fear to those who do what is right. Therefore, the righteous hide themselves. Interestingly, "*the righteous increase*," not necessarily when wicked rulers are replaced with righteous rulers, but simply when wicked rulers "*perish.*" The righteous are capable of prospering with or without civil authorities over them because of their reliance upon the providence of God (cf. 27:23-27) and submission to His rule. Yet righteous rulers are still able to be a blessing to the people of a nation (29:2; cf. 28:12).

Read: Proverbs 27:24

God's reign is eternal. Human rulers hold power for a short period of time by comparison. Therefore, all men – both in and out of positions of power – need to remember the limitations of civil authority and submit to the one with ultimate authority – God.

Related passages: Proverbs 30:29-31; 20:28; 25:2-3; 25:5

Instructions to Those in Government

Moving on from statements *about* government, we will now consider instructions in the book of Proverbs directed specifically toward those in power.

Read: Proverbs 8:15-16

The "*me*" of this passage is *Wisdom* (8:12). This wisdom is not a worldly wisdom but wisdom that comes from above. Those in positions of authority must not rely upon their own wisdom but seek after God's wisdom.

Read: Proverbs 29:4

Stability is desirable for a nation as it includes the conditions of peace (from threats without and within) and a freedom from want. This is good for the people, but is also good for the rulers as the people remain content under their rule. This stability is made possible through fairness and justice. A ruler must not be able to be bought, as this will overthrow the stability in the land.

Read: Proverbs 29:14

Too often, men will show kindness to those who they believe will be able to reciprocate. For those in positions of power, this means that they pay special regard to those who are rich, powerful, and influential; but the poor are often ignored. Rulers must pay attention to the poor and judge them *"with truth"* as this, not the neglect of the poor in favor of the rich, will cause his throne to be established.

Read: Proverbs 31:8-9

This passage is related to the one previously noted (29:14). Those who are unable to defend themselves must be protected by the civil authorities against those who would abuse them. But in all of this, the king must rule *justly* (29:4). The rights of the less fortunate must be defended. However, in defending the rights of the lowly against the rich and powerful, a ruler must not go to the other extreme – attack the rights of the rich in the name of the poor. The Law specifically stated: *"Nor shall you be partial to a poor man in his dispute"* (Exodus 23:3). Showing favoritism – for either the rich or the poor – is a perversion of justice. A ruler must *"defend the rights of the afflicted and needy"* without assaulting the rights of others.

Read: Proverbs 16:10-12

The statement, *"A divine decision is in the lips of the king,"* means that a king ought to rule in such a way that is in harmony with God's law. *"A just balance and scales belong to the Lord"* means that everything that is right, just, and fair is in harmony with His instructions. No human standard that is contrary to God's standard ought to be followed or enforced. Furthermore, when Solomon says, "*It is an abomination for kings to commit wicked acts,*" he is saying that those in authority are not above the law – either God's law or man's. Therefore, rulers must act *righteously* in the fear of God.

Read: Proverbs 14:28

Though it would be easy for a ruler to become arrogant because of his position, the wise man reminds him that his *glory* or *honour* (KJV) is only possible because of the people he rules. There are two implications to this. First, without the loyalty of the people, those in power cannot rule, which leads to their downfall. This means that for one to effectively rule over the long-term, he must do so with the consent of the governed. Second, without the life of the people, those in power cannot rule. Therefore, being in a position of civil authority demands that one protect the people from those who would do harm to them.

Read: Proverbs 17:26

We have already noticed the responsibility of rulers to punish evildoers (20:8, 26). However, they must take care not to punish the righteous along with the wicked. Peter would later explain the primary responsibility of civil authorities: "*For the punishment of evildoers and the praise of those who do right*" (1 Peter 2:14). A sloppy execution of punishment that affects the righteous is not good. Those who are righteous and upright should not be fined, struck down, or otherwise harmed by those in power.

Read: Proverbs 28:4

It is assumed in this verse that the law under consideration is just and in harmony with divine precepts. Though there may be some ungodly laws that are created to praise and reward the wicked, those laws that are in harmony with the will of God will be opposed to the wicked. Therefore, if a ruler sides with the wicked, he has forsaken every legitimate law that agrees with divine law. A ruler who fears God and understands the importance of governing according to divine precepts will *"strive (contend, KJV) with"* the wicked.

Related passages: Proverbs 16:13; 17:7; 29:12; 28:15-16

Our Responsibility Toward Government

Most men will not find themselves in government, but subject to governing authorities. Therefore, it is important that we understand what our responsibility and attitude should be toward those in power.

Read: Proverbs 24:21

In considering the danger of bad friends, we already noticed that trouble comes when one associates with *"those who are given to change."* Sometimes change is necessary, such as when one is changing from a state of wickedness to a state of righteousness. But this verse is warning about those with a rebellious attitude who want change for the sake of change. Some civil authorities will roughly follow God's instructions for them. Others will completely reject God's will for them. Naturally, the righteous man will want stability with the good rulers and change with the evil rulers. However, some are not content no matter who is in charge. They want change when the wicked are in power and when the righteous are in power. We are not to keep company with those who have such a rebellious attitude.

Read: Proverbs 22:11

This verse assumes that the king is righteous himself so that he values such qualities. But regardless of the character of the king, we must act with honor and integrity. This is the only right way to gain favor with those in authority.

Those who are righteous will take note of it and respond with kindness.

Read: Proverbs 20:2

The king has the power to do harm to those he desires to punish. This may be done properly (punishing evildoers – 20:26) or improperly (oppressing the righteous along with the wicked – 17:26). Regardless of the reason for the wrath that comes from those in power, we should do as Paul told the brethren in Thessalonica: "*Make it your ambition to lead a quiet life*" (1 Thessalonians 4:11). We should not be looking for trouble but should strive to conduct our lives in such a way that those in power – whether righteous or wicked – will leave us alone.

Read: Proverbs 23:1-3

This passage warns us that not everything that is offered to us by those in power is helpful or good for us. Therefore, if the government offers us *anything*, before agreeing to accept it, we need to carefully consider the potential ramifications of our acceptance. There may be times in which it would be better to refuse what is offered to us than to accept what is offered along with whatever strings are attached to it.

Read: Proverbs 29:26

This is possibly the most important verse to remember in the book of Proverbs about our attitude toward civil authorities. Many people seek the favor of rulers because they see these leaders as holding the power of life or death over them (cf. 16:14-15). Yet we must remember that "*justice for man comes from the Lord.*" Any justice from civil authorities only comes as they comply with the will of God. Any injustice from civil authorities will one day be made right by God as He is over all, even those who rule over us in this life. Rather than looking to civil authority as our deliverer and the standard of righteousness, we need to look to God for these things. We must never forget the surpassing greatness of God and the inferiority and comparative weakness of human rulers.

Related passage: Proverbs 25:6-7

Questions on Lesson 13

1. If 14:34 specifically applies to individuals, then in what way can it also apply to government?

2. Explain the connection between sin and many princes (28:2).

3. What is meant by the phrase, "*It is the glory of God to conceal a matter, but the glory of kings to search out a matter*" (25:2)?

4. What is necessary in order to give "*stability to the land*" (29:4)?

5. Why is it "*not good to fine the righteous*" (17:26)?

6. What warning is given in 23:1-3 about accepting what is offered to us by a ruler?

7. Though "*many seek the ruler's favor*," what is the source of true justice (29:26)?

Lesson 14

The Application: God

Key verses: Proverbs 8:22; 30:5-6; 1:7; 14:2, 26-27; 15:3; 3:5-8; 18:10; 21:3

The final point of application in our study of Proverbs has to do with God and our relationship to Him. The entire book of Proverbs has been a discussion of the wisdom that comes from above. Of course, the source of this wisdom is God Himself. But without understanding God and our place before Him, it would be difficult for us to find sufficient reason to trust that His way is best and live our lives according to it. Therefore, we must understand God to fully understand the importance of the wisdom contained in this book.

About God

Read: Proverbs 8:22

Wisdom is speaking in this verse. The verses that follow mention God as being *eternal* (8:23) and our *Creator* (8:24-31). The wisdom that has been discussed in the book of Proverbs belongs to Him. He did not have to acquire wisdom as we do. He possessed wisdom before the world was even formed.

Read: Proverbs 21:30

Because wisdom belongs to God (8:22), He is the standard. Therefore, we cannot successfully challenge Him. Job made this same point about God: "*If one wished to dispute with Him, he could not answer Him once in a thousand times*" (Job 9:3).

Read: Proverbs 30:5-6

The word of God has stood the test of time, and man cannot improve upon it. Therefore, one who would attempt to improve upon God's word by adding to it will be "*proved a liar.*" Not only is the word of God *right*, but it is *complete*, making additions to it unnecessary. Being complete as it is, His word as a "*shield*" is able to provide the perfect defense and protection for "*those who take refuge in Him.*"

Read: Proverbs 20:12

God is the Creator (cf. 8:22-31; Genesis 1:1). But some today, in a foolish attempt to harmonize the fact that God is Creator with the godless theory of evolution, have suggested that God created the universe and set processes in motion that would lead to the evolution of life as we know it (theistic evolution). Yet God did not create the matter and conditions whereby man would eventually evolve from lower forms of life, which evolved themselves from still lower forms of life. Instead, the wise man affirms that God made "*the hearing ear and the seeing eye*" of man.

Read: Proverbs 15:29

This is similar to what Solomon's father David wrote in the Psalms: "*The eyes of the Lord are toward the righteous and His ears are open to their cry. The face of the Lord is against evildoers, to cut off the memory of them from the earth*" (Psalm 34:15-16; cf. 1 Peter 3:12). While Solomon mentions God being "*far from the wicked,*" David went further and said that God is "*against evildoers.*" God, in His justice, will not allow the wicked to go unpunished. Though He may leave them on their own for a time, He will eventually punish them. On the other hand, the righteous enjoy a continued state of God's kindness and watchfulness.

Related passages: Proverbs 19:21; 22:12

Fear God

Read: Proverbs 1:7

Fear is inseparably connected with obedience (cf. Ecclesiastes 12:13; Acts 10:35). Yet in order to obey, one must have knowledge about what to obey. The two sides of fear – respect for God and terror of God – motivate one to find out what God desires of him so that he can obey the Lord's will.

Read: Proverbs 24:21

We have already cited this verse in connection with friendships and government. It is necessary to include it here as well. We are not to have a heart of rebellion but one of submission to God, rooted in a healthy fear of Him.

Read: Proverbs 14:2

The proof of one fearing the Lord is walking uprightly. Without practicing righteousness, one cannot claim that he truly fears God. Jesus expressed the same principle of obedience proving one's devotion to God: "*If you love Me, you will keep My commandments*" (John 14:15). If we do not keep the Lord's commandments, our claim that we love Him is baseless. In the same way, if we do not practice righteousness, our claim that we fear God is baseless. If we are "*perverse in* [our] *ways*" (KJV), we are showing our contempt for God and proving that "*there is no fear of God before* [our] *eyes*" (Psalm 36:1; cf. Romans 3:18).

Read: Proverbs 8:13

Many people want to claim to be religious and have faith in God, yet they tolerate, accept, and, in some cases, even practice those things which are evil. If we truly fear God, we will "*hate evil*" as He also does (cf. 6:16-19).

Read: Proverbs 14:26-27

The wise man is not saying that one who fears God has a right to become arrogant. This is not about *arrogance*, but *confidence*. If we fear God, we will understand the need to obey Him and then will actually do it. When we know that we are serving the Lord, we can be confident knowing that we are obeying the truth (His word), that we are avoiding the consequences of sin (*"the snares of death"*), and that we have a hope of a reward from Him (*"a fountain of life"*).

Read: Proverbs 23:17

There will be times when it seems as though sinners are better off than we are. During these times, we may be tempted to envy them. But we must not do this. As noted in the previous verse, one who fears the Lord is better off than one who does not, regardless of the earthly peace and prosperity enjoyed by the godless person (15:16). The future of the one who fears God is better than the future of the wicked man. Therefore, we must continually live in the fear of God so that we can please Him in all things.

* * *

Understanding who God is and what He has done should be reason enough to fear (respect) Him. We are to have a balanced fear of the Lord (respect and terror). So that we will be motivated to obey, we must remember our accountability before Him as we will stand before Him in judgment.

Read: Proverbs 5:21; 15:3

God is omniscient – He sees and knows all (cf. Hebrews 4:13). There is nowhere to go to hide from the Lord as His *"eyes...are in every place."* There is nothing we can do that would be beyond His awareness, as our *"ways...are before* [His] *eyes...and He watches all* [our] *paths."* Rather than try to hide from the Lord, we should strive to be numbered among those who are good, rather than among those who are evil.

Read: Proverbs 15:11; 20:27

Before telling us, "*All things are open and laid bare to the eyes of Him with whom we have to do,*" the Hebrew writer said, "*The word of God is...able to judge the thoughts and intentions of the heart*" (Hebrews 4:12-13). God knows our thoughts and what is in our hearts. It is certainly true that no one among our fellow men can know our thoughts and intentions. Paul wrote, "*For who among men knows the thoughts of a man except the spirit of the man which is in him?*" (1 Corinthians 2:11). But God is different from man. He "*forms the spirit of man within him*" (Zechariah 12:1). Therefore, though we may be able to hide "*the thoughts and intentions of the heart*" from others, it is impossible to hide them from God.

Read: Proverbs 22:2

Though men may not treat the rich and poor as equals, they are equal before God. God is their Maker. Both have a common origin, and they have been made "*in the image of God*" (Genesis 1:27; cf. Acts 17:26). They also both have a common future. When they die, "*the dust will return to the earth as it was, and the spirit will return to God who gave it*" (Ecclesiastes 12:7). No matter what our temporary circumstances are in this life, we will one day meet our Maker and will have to give an account for what we have done in our lives (cf. Hebrews 9:27; 2 Corinthians 5:10).

Read: Proverbs 17:3

The purpose of the refining pot and the furnace was to remove from the silver and gold any impurities that might have been present. God tests our hearts in the same way through the standard found in His revealed word. The goal for us – just as it is with silver and gold – is *purity*. As He tests our hearts, He is determining whether we are worthy of a reward or not.

Read: Proverbs 21:2

Everyone does what he believes to be right. Of course, what one believes to be right is not necessarily going to be right (cf. 14:12; 16:25; Jeremiah 10:23). If everyone were a standard to himself, then all would be justified. But we answer to a higher power – God. He *"weighs the hearts"* (cf. 17:3) to determine whether or not we can stand justified before Him.

Related passages: 16:1-7; 19:23; 15:16; 24:12

Trust God

Read: Proverbs 3:5-8

Solomon's primary point in this passage is that we must put our trust in God, rather than thinking we can find the path of wisdom apart from Him. But it is important that we put our trust in Him *completely* – with all our hearts (3:5) and in all our ways (3:6). If we do this, *"He will make* [our] *paths straight."* This does not mean that whatever we do will be right. We can still choose to do what is wrong. Instead, Solomon's point is that God will direct our steps to whatever degree we acknowledge Him and trust in His ways. We must trust in God in fear (3:7) – knowing that God has the power to destroy us but will not do so as long as we obey Him and *"turn away from evil."* Doing this will lead to our being blessed by God.

Read: Proverbs 16:33

This verse does not mean that everything that happens or is decided has been foreordained by God. Solomon also wrote, *"Time and chance overtake them all"* (Ecclesiastes 9:11). The casting of lots was a practice done under the Old Law for matters which required a divine decision (cf. Leviticus 16:7-10). The apostles cast lots to determine who would replace Judas in their number

(Acts 1:23-26). It did not produce a random outcome, but a divinely-decreed outcome (it would *"show which one...You have chosen"* – Acts 1:24). It eliminated the influence of man in the decision, thus requiring man to put his trust in God for the decision. Though we should not expect God to reveal His will to us through the casting of lots today, we should trust Him enough to look to what He has revealed – His word – to guide us in our lives.

Read: Proverbs 18:10

There is safety and protection to be found in the Lord. However, this safety is only enjoyed by those who *run to Him* so that they might be protected. We cannot stubbornly refuse to follow God and expect Him to be with us.

Related passages: Proverbs 29:25; 20:22

Pleasing God

Read: Proverbs 21:3

The type of sacrifice mentioned in this verse is the sacrifice that would be offered for sin. God has always given His people an avenue whereby they could obtain forgiveness for their sins. Yet this avenue of forgiveness – whether the sacrifices under the Old Law or the prayers we offer to God today (1 John 1:9; Acts 8:22) – is not to be abused. Though an avenue of forgiveness exists, the first priority of God's people ought to be to avoid sin in the first place (cf. 1 John 2:1). This is why Solomon says that practicing *"righteousness and justice"* is preferable to one needing to seek forgiveness. It is as Samuel told Saul: *"Has the Lord as much delight in burnt offerings and sacrifices as in obeying the voice of the Lord? Behold, to obey is better than sacrifice, and to heed than the fat of rams"* (1 Samuel 15:22).

Read: Proverbs 28:9

If one does not obey the Lord, thereby demonstrating a lack of respect for Him, he has no right to expect the Lord to heed him when he prays. Furthermore, the wise man says that the prayer of one who refuses to obey God "*is an abomination.*" It is not just that God *ignores* the prayers of the disobedient. These prayers are *offensive* to Him. David also spoke of God's active opposition to the wicked as opposed to some divine indifference: "*The eyes of the Lord are toward the righteous and His ears are open to their cry. The face of the Lord is against evildoers, to cut off the memory of them from the earth*" (Psalm 34:15-16; cf. 1 Peter 3:12).

Read: Proverbs 15:8-9

Just as the prayer of the disobedient is offensive to God (cf. 28:9), "*the sacrifice of the wicked*" is offensive as well (cf. 21:3). On the other hand, God delights in "*the prayer of the upright.*" He wants man to come to Him in prayer, but man must make a sincere effort to please Him. "*He loves one who pursues righteousness.*" The fact that this is a pursuit does not mean that righteousness is unattainable, but rather that righteousness is something which must be continually sought. It requires *action* on man's part; as the apostle John wrote, "*The one who practices righteousness is righteous, just as He is righteous*" (1 John 3:4). But "*the way of the wicked*" – his sinful actions and the ungodly direction of his life – is offensive to the Lord.

Read: Proverbs 15:26

In the verses above, Solomon has shown God's contempt for the prayers, sacrifices, and actions of the wicked (28:9; 15:8-9). This verse goes further in saying that "*evil plans are an abomination to the Lord.*" God is aware of more than what is visible (our ways, 15:9) and what is directed specifically toward Him (prayers, 28:9; sacrifices, 15:8). Being omniscient, He is aware of our thoughts. If our thoughts are wicked, they are "*an abomination*" to Him. The second phrase of this verse is different in the King James Version. While the New American Standard translation seems to be simply describing a characteristic of *"pleasant words"* (that they are pure), the King James Version makes a clearer contrast with the plans/thoughts of the wicked in the first part of the verse: *"But the words of the pure are pleasant words"* (KJV). God delights in those who are pure and upright. These characteristics will be seen even in one's speech.

Read: Proverbs 11:20

This verse contains the same thought as some of the verses previously considered. Those who are corrupt in their heart are offensive to God. Those who obey Him and follow the path of wisdom are pleasing to Him.

Related passage: Proverbs 17:15

Questions on Lesson 14

1. Why is one condemned for adding to God's word (30:6)?

2. Why is *"the fear of the Lord...the beginning of knowledge"* (1:7)?

3. Why is there *"strong confidence"* in the fear of the Lord (14:26)?

4. What is the common bond between the rich and the poor (22:2)?

5. What is *"the lot cast into the lap"* and how is *"its every decision...from the Lord"* (16:33)?

6. Why is doing righteousness and justice preferred by God more than offering sacrifice (21:3; cf. 1 Samuel 15:22)?

7. Why does God not accept the prayer of the wicked (28:9)?

Conclusion

Throughout this study, we have seen how God expects His people to grow in wisdom – not wisdom that is of the world, but wisdom that comes from above. As we have gone through this study, we have divided the material in the book of Proverbs into four sections:

1. **The *appeal* of wisdom** – God has not hidden His wisdom so that we cannot find it. He offers it to us. Solomon describes wisdom as *inviting* us to take hold of it. This invitation is open to all, not just to an elite few.

2. **The *appreciation* of wisdom** – When God calls us to take hold of His wisdom, He does not do so without giving us the reasons why it is good for us to pursue wisdom. There are blessings that come from following wisdom and negative consequences that come from rejecting wisdom.

3. **The *acquisition* of wisdom** – Once we recognize the *appeal* of wisdom and understand the reasons why we should *appreciate* wisdom, we then need to know how to *acquire* wisdom. With diligence and a proper attitude on our part, we can gain the wisdom that God offers.

4. **The *application* of wisdom** – Wisdom is not just about what we *know*, but what we *do*. Therefore, the bulk of the book of Proverbs focuses on how we are to *apply* wisdom. This will cover every area of our lives – home, work, society, and religion.

Our pursuit and application of wisdom is something that must be done throughout our lives. Our present and future happiness depends upon our remembering this fact.

"My son, eat honey for it is good, yes, the honey from the comb is sweet to your taste; know that wisdom is thus for your soul; if you find it, then there will be a future, and your hope will not be cut off" (24:13-14).

Our *souls* – our entire being, including our existence beyond this life – is benefited by wisdom. By following wisdom, we can look forward in hope to a future reward from God. But in order for this hope to be realized, we must not turn back from following wisdom.

"Hear, O sons, the instruction of a father, and give attention that you may gain understanding, for I give you sound teaching; do not abandon my instruction" (4:1-2).

"Acquire wisdom! Acquire understanding! Do not forget nor turn away from the words of my mouth" (4:5).

"My son, give attention to my words; incline your ear to my sayings. Do not let them depart from your sight; keep them in the midst of your heart" (4:20-21).

"Let your eyes look directly ahead and let your gaze be fixed straight in front of you. Watch the path of your feet and all your ways will be established. Do not turn to the right nor to the left; turn your foot from evil" (4:25-27).

Never forget the *appeal* of wisdom, in which God invites you to take hold of the wisdom that has been His since the beginning.

Never forget the need to *appreciate* wisdom, remembering the blessings that come from following wisdom and the pitfalls that come from rejecting it.

Never forget the need to *acquire* wisdom, in humility seeking diligently to obtain it.

Never forget the need to *apply* wisdom, following the will of God in every area and at every age of your life.

I pray that this study has been helpful to you, encouraging you toward more faithful service to God.

Made in the USA
Columbia, SC
10 April 2022

58776381R00087